# GERMAN SAILORS

—————— *in* ——————

# HAMPTON ROADS

*A World War I Story at the Norfolk Navy Yard*

*Gregory J. Hansard*

THE
History
PRESS

Published by The History Press
Charleston, SC
www.historypress.net

*Front cover, top*: Library of Congress; *bottom*: Portsmouth Naval Shipyard Museum.
*Back cover, top*: Portsmouth Naval Shipyard Museum; *bottom*: Library of Congress.

First published 2018

Manufactured in the United States

ISBN 9781625859525

Library of Congress Control Number: 2017960101

*These lights, the first signs of shore I had seen in many a day, were so welcome they seemed like home. Behind those lights was a haven of safety, a great nation, friendly to both sides in the war, and now our sole hope of protection.*

—*Count Alfred von Niezychowski, officer of the SMS* Kronprinz Wilhelm

*For Erin, with love*
*Thank you for your unending support and confidence.*

# CONTENTS

Foreword, by Diane L. Cripps                                                      9
Preface                                                                          13

Chapter 1. "A Warlike Appearance in Hampton Roads"                               15
Chapter 2. The Case of the *William P. Frye*
    and the Kaiser's Courteous Pirates                       38
Chapter 3. German Sailors in Hampton Roads:
    Tourism, Beer and the Tiny Village                        48
Chapter 4. The Activities of Interned Sailors:
    Baseball, Religion and Parties                            66
Chapter 5. The Problems of Internment:
    Escapes, Passes and the Saga of the *Eclipse*             79
Chapter 6. A Change in the Guard                                                 90

Epilogue                                                                        103
Notes                                                                           111
Index                                                                           123
About the Author                                                                127

# FOREWORD

*R*oadstead is an old word for a safe, sheltered stretch of water connected to the open sea, outside a harbor, where ships can ride at anchor. It is derived from an even older term, *roads*, designating such a location in an era when waterborne transportation was more important than overland travel. Most roadsteads around the world have long histories as centers of transportation and naval operations.

Hampton Roads (a region in southeast Virginia as well as an enormous safe harbor) is a textbook example. This roadstead at the southern end of the Chesapeake Bay—and the seemingly endless rivers and creeks that perforate the coastlines here—attracted some of history's earliest mariners looking for shelter from storms, ice and enemies. The communities that cropped up along the banks of these waterways built their economies and reputations on their connection to the sea.

It is no wonder that when the young United States was looking for a place to develop its infant navy at the beginning of the nineteenth century, it purchased an existing shipyard in Hampton Roads—specifically in Portsmouth. Those sixteen acres on the banks of the southern branch of the Elizabeth River developed into today's Norfolk Naval Shipyard, the U.S. Navy's oldest and largest shipyard.

Portsmouth and the shipyard grew up together, and their stories intertwine and connect with each other. No matter where you delve into the past here, you'll find Portsmouth, the navy, the shipyard and the sea itself playing equal roles in the tales that define local history. Some of those tales, like many involving the sea, are mysterious, thought-provoking and odd.

A little more than a century after the establishment of the navy yard, a tale odd and charming in equal measure—the appearance of the German Village at Norfolk Navy Yard (as it was then known)—offers us a peek at a strange political moment when the United States teetered on the brink of entering a global war. Before the horrors of the First World War settled into Americans' minds and sent their sons Over There, there was the peculiar period of neutrality declared by President Woodrow Wilson. In a nation of immigrants, the president knew that keeping Americans from choosing sides in a war involving so many countries would prove difficult. As the Central Powers' aggressive war efforts reached farther and farther around the globe, neutrality became harder and harder to maintain.

In Hampton Roads, the appearance of two hulking German merchant raiders in a neutral port should perhaps have struck fear into the hearts of local citizens. Instead, it produced enthusiastic news coverage and curiosity. When the ships' captains chose internment over facing the open ocean (and Allied vessels waiting offshore), they had to be transferred to a government facility: Norfolk Navy Yard in Portsmouth.

Neutrality and internment meant that the hundreds of German sailors making up the ships' crews were unable to fight and were stuck in a foreign land. Human nature being endlessly resourceful, the Germans turned their sidelined energy into a tourist attraction: a "German Village" cobbled together from scrap materials and ingenuity on empty shipyard property next to the docked ships. Portsmouth residents, as well as visitors from farther afield, ate it up.

At the Portsmouth Naval Shipyard Museum in Portsmouth, Virginia, we have a few ephemeral pieces of this incongruous moment in local and American history, when what should have been a feared potential enemy was welcomed with open arms. Postcards, private photographs and even a piece or two of silver from the German ships are touchstones of this unique event. Museums excel at telling stories through artifacts. However, while we might have been able to look at these items and marvel at this story, we did not have any firsthand accounts of the German sailors themselves. How did they interact with the local citizens? The story of the German Village has been told many times in Portsmouth and neighboring Norfolk. But it has never been told from the perspective of the sailors themselves. Until now.

Museum curators like to think we have the corner on history and the material culture it left behind. But the best history drills all the way down to a point beyond the artifacts, where we can access insights into human nature. We get a glimpse into the emotions and perceptions of the people of the past. At that level, perhaps we can try to make sense of these interned German sailors, as well as the people who eagerly paid their admission to the German Village. After a few short months, the sailors were taken prisoner, the village disappeared and the tourists had to be disappointed. There was a war on.

A roadstead is a watery crossroads where the cultures, ideas and ironies of history intersect, leaving the lessons of the past in their wake. As you delve into this ironic tale, I wish you the pleasantries of discovery, the challenges of paradox and the surprises at what the mirror of history reflects back at us.

Diane L. Cripps
Curator of History,
Portsmouth Museums/Portsmouth Naval Shipyard Museum
Portsmouth, Virginia
June 2017

# PREFACE

I worked at the Virginia Historical Society, a research library and museum located in Richmond, Virginia, for twelve years. From 2008 to 2011, I served as an assistant editor for its scholarly journal and members' newsletter. One of my favorite jobs was not fact-checking the articles or indexing an issue of the *Virginia Magazine of History and Biography* (as much fun as that sounds); it was finding a mystery photograph for the newsletter. One day, I was searching through the postcard collection, trying to find something that would stump our readers, and I came across an image of jovial German sailors onboard a ship in Hampton Roads. I was excited and thought I had found an image to fool our readers. My next test was to check with the curator of prints and photographs. If I could stump him, then I could fool our readers. I proudly entered his office and asked him to identify the scene. He quickly responded, "Well, that's the German sailors who built the tiny village in Hampton Roads during World War I." But that was all he could tell me. I was initially disappointed that I couldn't use this image for our mystery photo, but I was intrigued at the story. I wanted to know more.

This led me down a path at the U.S. National Archives and Records Administration, where I discovered eighteen months of correspondence between the German captains and the U.S. government, along with endless amounts of miscellaneous manuscripts that ranged from Pabst Blue Ribbon receipts and family request passes to detailed descriptions of missing sailors (even drawings of their tattoos). Long days at the Library of Virginia scrolling through almost two years of newspaper coverage from the *Virginian-Pilot and the Norfolk Landmark* gave a clear picture of the German sailors' activities according to the local community. I tracked down rare photographs and postcards from the various archives that showcased the German Village, the sailors' ships and their interactions with American citizens. The Portsmouth Naval Shipyard Museum has several hidden gems related to the sailors, including a copy of the sailors' newspaper, the *Kolonie-Anzeiger*. All of these wonderful sources provided the evidence to tell the unique and perplexing story of eight hundred German sailors' internment in a Virginia maritime community during World War I.

I would like to thank several people who were instrumental in helping me produce this book. First, I am forever in debt to my editor and dear friend, Nelson Lankford. Without his assistance, this project would not be complete. His dedication and encouragement moved this narrative forward. I also had a tremendous amount of help from my commissioning editor at The History Press, Kate Jenkins, and production editor Rick Delaney. Their organization and project management helped keep this publication on track.

Others who helped with this project were Stephen Rockenbach at Virginia State University, Jamison Davis and Troy Wilkinson at the Virginia Historical Society, Troy Valos at the Norfolk Public Library, Peggie Haile McPhillips at the City of Norfolk, Diane L. Cripps at the Portsmouth Naval Shipyard Museum, Marcus W. Robbins at the Norfolk Naval Shipyard, M. Clayton Farrington at the Hampton Roads Naval Museum, Allen Cutchin and Jane Pellegrino at the Naval Medical Center Portsmouth, Suse Field, who assisted with translation, and Michael and Alicia Hohl, who provided comfortable lodging and gourmet meals during my trips to Norfolk. I would also like to thank my parents, Rick and Linda, for their unwavering support and love.

Above all, I'd like to thank my wife, Erin. Her belief in me is what gave me the strength and determination to complete this book.

# 1

# "A Warlike Appearance in Hampton Roads"

Smoke poured out of the two large funnels, and the propellers of the SMS *Prinz Eitel Friedrich* turned for over an hour as the young, poised German captain debated when he would make his daring dash back to sea. "You may miss me anytime," Korvettenkapitän Max T. Thierichens explained to hundreds of eager visitors who had come to catch a glimpse of the famous German raider that had sunk eleven merchant ships during its seven-month voyage from Tsingtao, China, to Virginia.[1] The raider that once wrought havoc on merchant ships now sat in Newport News, a neutral port on the Virginia coast, awaiting fuel and repairs before it could depart again. Thierichens, an enthusiastic and confident captain with a stout stature and unwavering eyes, expressed his feelings about leaving to the crowd. "I hate to go," he explained, "but duty comes first of all and besides we all have our mission to fill."[2]

The *Eitel* was one among several merchant ships and passenger liners that the German navy transformed into armed surface raiders at the outset of World War I in August 1914. Outfitted with guns and supplies and given a full crew of 402 men, they were ordered to sink any merchant vessels carrying contraband to the Allies. Thierichens told the enthusiastic crowd that he had not slept well before reaching port. According to the captain, "It was always the wireless had picked up something. Somebody was after us and they would wake me up to tell me."[3]

After running low on fuel and provisions, Thierichens had entered Hampton Roads under the cover of darkness. The *Eitel* had successfully

PRINZ EITEL FREDERICK.                    PHOTO BY UNDERWOOD & UNDERWOOD

**CARRANZA FORCES DRIVEN SOUTHWARD**

Report Of Result Of Clash Near Queretaro—Villa Army Defeated Near Tampico

HUERTA SAID TO BE EN ROUTE TO NEW YORK

El Paso, Tex., April 7.—The Villa and Obregon forces have clashed between Queretaro and Irapuato, according to a telegram from the scene of the fighting received here tonight. It was said that the Carranza forces after 24 hours fighting were driven some distance to the south, their return to Queretaro being cut off.

**Villa Army Defeated**

Washington, April 7.—Complete defeat of the Villa army moving against Tampico was claimed in a message from Tampico dated yesterday, receiv-

*Left*: When the war began, Max T. Thierichens was transferred from command of the *Luchs* gunboat to the *Eitel*, where he was now in charge of more than 400 crew members. *Norfolk Public Library, Norfolk, Virginia.*

*Below and opposite*: Many of the crew members wore colorful *Tiger* and *Luchs* ribbons on their hats. The SMS *Tiger* and SMS *Luchs* were two German gunboats that patrolled the waters around Tsingtao before World War I. Once the war began, sailors from these gunboats were ordered to board the *Eitel*. *Hampton Roads Naval Museum.*

slipped past Allied ships and had made it to the neutral waters of the United States. The German captain's nightmares ceased for the time being, but the uncertainty for the local community and the U.S. government had just begun.[4]

According to international law, no belligerent vessel could use a neutral port as a base for military operations. It was allowed one day for maintenance and fuel, unless granted additional time for further repairs to be made. After the twenty-four hours expired, it must either leave or become interned. The reason for this rule, according to the *American Journal of International Law*, was "so that neither it nor its crew may take further part in the war progress."[5] Article 24 of the Convention Concerning the Rights and Duties of Neutral Powers in Naval War states that once a vessel enters a neutral port, sailors must stay within the neutral territory or on their ship. Further restrictions can also be enforced by the neutral nation. The officers and men will be "left at liberty on giving their word not to quit the neutral area without permission."[6] These regulations attempted to keep a nonaligned country out of war. How would the nation respond if Thierichens left Hampton Roads?

Built in 1904 as a luxury liner for Norddeutscher Lloyd (North German Lloyd), the *Eitel* served as a commerce raider during the war and now sat anchored in Newport News. *Library of Congress.*

The arrival of the German ship in Hampton Roads on March 9, 1915, startled not only the maritime community but also the U.S. government. On March 10, Washington sent Lieutenant Commander Frank H. Brumby and Rear Admiral Bradley A. Fiske to inspect the *Eitel*. They reported that Thierichens thought it might take more than three weeks to restore the ship to working condition, with repairs to the propellers, rudder and boilers.[7] Only when the maintenance was completed could the crew return to sea. Along with the drama created by the anticipated departure of the *Eitel*, there was another issue regarding one of the ship's victims that greatly concerned the United States.

The *William P. Frye*, a four-masted American merchant ship, had left Seattle bound for England carrying a cargo of wheat. The vessel was intercepted by the *Eitel* on January 27, 1915. After Thierichens boarded the *Frye*, he found the wheat cargo and said that foodstuffs bound for Britain were considered contraband. The German captain's decision to sink the ship and the vessel's freight complicated U.S. and German relations for the next several months. When the *Eitel* entered U.S. waters, it had twenty-five members of the *Frye*'s crew onboard. The *William P. Frye* was the first American ship destroyed by German aggression during World War I, and the attacker now sought refuge in its victim's homeland.

Thierichens was not concerned about U.S. retaliation for the sinking of the *Frye*, but he was worried about the French and British taking revenge. The *Eitel*'s successful navigation into the Virginia port through the blockade was an embarrassing exposure of Allied naval ineffectiveness. The British and French did not want to make the same mistake twice, so they increased guard of the Virginia Capes by adding three warships.[8] The danger for Captain Thierichens was not only if he left port but also if he stayed in Hampton Roads. It was not unheard of for Allied ships to attack German ships docked in a neutral territory.

On August 26, 1914, the German converted battle cruiser SMS *Kaiser Wilhelm der Große* was refueling off the coast of northwest Africa when it was attacked by the British cruiser HMS *High Flyer*. Britain ignored the raider's claim of operating in neutral waters by attacking the auxiliary cruiser in the colony of Rio de Oro.[9] Surprised and outgunned, the *Kaiser* had little chance of survival. The vessel was badly damaged, scuttled and then abandoned by the crew. It was the first German converted passenger ship sunk during the war.

There were other instances of British violations of neutrality during the war. On March 14, 1915, HMS *Glasgow* and HMS *Kent* spotted the German

The Battle of Rio de Oro occurred on August 26, 1914, when HMS *High Flyer* attacked SMS *Kaiser Wilhelm der Große* in the neutral Spanish territory of Rio de Oro. *Library of Congress.*

ship SMS *Dresden* at anchor in Cumberland Bay off the coast of Chile. When the *Dresden* saw the British ships approaching, the cruiser raised its guns. The commander of the British detachment, Captain John Luce, saw this as an act of aggression and ordered the *Glasgow* to fire on the *Dresden*. The German ship quickly responded with a salvo of its own. After a few minutes of exchanges, the *Dresden*, crippled and smoking, was forced to raise the white flag. The Chilean government bitterly protested the violation of its neutrality. It was upset at the Germans for firing while docked and the British for the property damage from their shells. The British commander paid compensation to the Chileans, but German losses had to be settled through diplomatic channels. Luce had orders to destroy the *Dresden* wherever it was found and was told to let the diplomats sort it out later. On April 15, Britain sent a "full and ample apology" to the Chilean government for the damage and for the sinking of *Dresden*, but the British still protested that the German ship had not accepted internment and had its colors flying and guns trained.[10]

Being attacked in port by the Allies was not the only possible outcome for the crew of the *Eitel*. The U.S. government had the power to destroy belligerent vessels if they attempted to leave U.S. territory without gaining clearance. One example involved the German merchant ship *Odenwald*. The vessel had remained anchored at San Juan, Puerto Rico, since the beginning of the war, but in March 1915, when it attempted to leave without clearance, it was met with gunfire from U.S. coastal positions at El Morro Fort on the northwest islet of San Juan. After several shells exploded near the *Odenwald*, the ship was forced back into harbor and remained interned until the United States entered the war. The vessel was then taken over by the U.S. Navy in 1917 and recommissioned the USS *Newport News*.[11]

Despite the dangers, Thierichens made it clear that, once he arrived in Hampton Roads, he was not intent on staying. He was disappointed with waiting and not serving his country. "You have no idea what it means to lie idle here, when we know they are fighting at home," he explained.[12] Even when Thierichens and his crew were chasing merchant ships trading with the enemy, he felt that they were missing out. They read about the big battles in the paper but never came close to one during their voyage, except the Battle of Coronel.

That engagement occurred on November 1, 1914, off the coast of Chile and pitted British rear admiral Sir Christopher Cradock against German vice admiral Count Maximilian von Spee. The numbers were overwhelmingly in Spee's favor, and the results showed. The German

Germans ships entered Valparaiso Harbor after their victory at the Battle of Coronel, in which more than fifteen hundred British sailors lost their lives, including Rear Admiral Sir Christopher Cradock. (The historic Cradock neighborhood in Portsmouth is named after the rear admiral.) *Library of Congress.*

Norman R. Hamilton served as the collector of customs of Virginia from 1914 to 1922. The Portsmouth native and former newspaper reporter met regularly with the German captains. *Library of Congress.*

squadron of two armored cruisers and three auxiliary cruisers easily defeated the British squadron consisting of two armored cruisers, one auxiliary cruiser and one light cruiser.[13] Thierichens revealed, "I didn't see that, but I heard it."[14] He was with his radio operator and heard the German ship SMS *Scharnhorst* give the order to fire once it spotted the British. By the end of the battle, casualties for the British were devastating—1,570 killed, including Cradock—while the German casualties were only three wounded.[15] War stories like that of the Battle of Coronel reminded Thierichens of how important it was to return to the seas. He had made it to Virginia chased by six warships, and he thought it would not be difficult to elude five enemy ships on the way out. Although the German captain was eager to continue his mission, he would have to wait for the U.S. government to give him clearance.

President Woodrow Wilson had issued a declaration of neutrality on August 4, 1914, asking Americans "to be impartial in thought as well as in action."[16] The situation in Hampton Roads threatened this neutrality. By March 19, 1915, Secretary of State Robert Lansing declared that the State Department would make no public information available regarding the *Eitel*. This was done to ensure that no tips were accidently or purposefully given to French or British agents.[17] Photography of the ship and sailors was also prohibited. One cameraman snapped pictures of the ship, but the U.S. Navy guards confiscated his camera and threw his plates into the water.[18] The German cruiser was guarded so tightly that even Virginia's collector of customs, Norman R. Hamilton, had difficulty getting to the ship.[19] Hamilton, tasked with organizing the departure of the German ship from Newport News, had to meet constantly with Thierichens. The captain apologized one day because of the difficulty. "Mr. Collector, I am sorry to put you to so much trouble," Thierichens told Hamilton. "You stay on the pier and I will come to you."[20]

THE HEADLINES OF THE *Virginian-Pilot and the Norfolk Landmark* greeted readers with a surprise on the morning of March 26, 1915. The paper exclaimed that "with the German auxiliary cruiser *Prinz Eitel Friedrich* apparently making preparations to sail and with three foreign warships off the Virginia Capes, Hampton Roads took on a real warlike appearance last night when the entire garrison of Fortress Monroe and Fort Wool were called to quarters."[21] This episode startled the maritime community and was the beginning of the entire country's focus on the sprint of the cruiser to the open seas. The uncertainty and importance of the situation prompted the *Richmond Times-Dispatch* to call the presence of the *Eitel* on the Virginia coast one of the most significant events that had occurred on North American soil during the war.

U.S. forces in Hampton Roads at Fort Monroe were in constant contact with Secretary of the Navy Josephus Daniels. For the next week, he was determined to make sure that neutrality was not jeopardized by a dash to sea by the German ship. Daniels mobilized several ships from Philadelphia and ordered the navy's reserve fleet to Hampton Roads to secure the situation. At first, the U.S. Navy had very little help to offer. A single Coast Guard cutter was the first to be ordered to investigate and enforce neutrality. Most of the Atlantic Fleet was near Puerto Rico on maneuvers and wouldn't return for another month, so several ships had to be called down to Hampton Roads from other U.S. ports. On March 27, 1915, Daniels ordered the battleship USS *Alabama* of the Atlantic Reserve Fleet to Hampton Roads from the Philadelphia Navy Yard. He believed that there needed to be one large ship on guard to support the subs and destroyers already on the Capes. His letter of March 27, 1915, explained that they must "proceed with U.S.S. *Alabama* [to] Hampton Roads temporary neutrality duty detail."[22]

These safety precautions were put in place to guard the *Eitel* when (or if) it left, as well as to guard it if any Allied ship attempted to harm it. Four more U.S. Navy subs were sent to Hampton Roads, and another ship was ordered to keep an eye on six German vessels near Boston. President Wilson wanted to avoid any confrontation that might lead to American involvement in the war.

Daniels also increased defensive fortifications by sending a marine patrol out onto the beach and piers at Old Point Comfort. Marine and coast guard

A 1921 map of Hampton Roads. Hampton Roads is both a body of water and a landmass. The area consists of parts of southeastern Virginia and northeastern North Carolina. The *Eitel* and *Wilhelm* first arrived in Newport News and were then moved to the Norfolk Navy Yard in Portsmouth. *Portsmouth Naval Shipyard Museum.*

*Left*: Josephus Daniels served as secretary of the navy from 1913 to 1921 under Woodrow Wilson. *Library of Congress.*

*Below*: The USS *Alabama*, an 11,565-ton Illinois class battleship, was called from training exercises to Norfolk to provide added protection during the potential departure of the *Eitel*. *Library of Congress.*

units set up ammunition, guns and searchlights at every shore battery.[23] The marines guarded against the threat of the *Eitel* leaving port, and the navy and coast guard intended to intercept the vessel before it could reach Allied ships. Washington ordered the commander in chief of the Atlantic Reserve Fleet to fire on the German cruiser if it left within twenty-four hours of any Allied ships.[24] The captain of the Coast Artillery Corps responded that they will take forcible action "if ordered by War Department."[25] The goal of the U.S. government was to guarantee neutrality at all costs. The Americans would either protect or destroy the German ship, depending on the circumstances. They could not let the *Eitel* break the Hague provision and bring America into a world war.

One of the rules of the Hague Convention of 1907 declared: "A belligerent warship may not leave a neutral port until twenty four hours after the departure of a merchant ship flying the flag of its adversary."[26] This international law is in place so that combative ships have enough time to clear the neutral territory limits before possible engagements. Daniels ordered the Newport News Shipbuilding & Dry Dock Company and the Norfolk Navy Yard in Portsmouth to "keep track of sailing of British, French, Russian, Japanese vessels" and to "use force if necessary."[27] Enforcing the Hague provision created economic problems, because the Hampton Roads haven had to hold up shipping for the *Eitel*. The Virginia Capes marked the entrance to three of the largest ports in the county—Newport News, Norfolk and Baltimore. There was very heavy traffic in shipments of grain, coal and horses. Over the course of a week, a typical schedule for the Norfolk Navy Yard included more than twenty British and French ships.[28] Any interference with the port would hurt the Hampton Roads shipping economy. A holdup would also hurt British and French interests, because their supplies would be delayed.

The British government had already claimed that the United States violated the Hague Conventions, because it allowed the *Eitel* to be cleaned and painted. The British argued that this helped to improve the ship's condition, allowing it to now steam faster than it could before. On April 5, the British consul in Norfolk complained that the U.S. government had allowed the *Eitel* to stay too long.[29] The presence of the German raider in U.S. territory generated tension between the British and American governments; if the *Eitel* left port, this dispute could lead to military action on the Virginia coast.

On April 1, 1915, Captain Thierichens checked the weather forecast but did not indicate whether or not he would go. He instructed his paymaster to pay all claims against the *Eitel* accrued during its stay. He alleged that, with

The German merchant raiders used a large amount of coal. The sailors loaded more than 1,600 tons of coal onto the *Eitel*. *Hampton Roads Naval Museum.*

his ship scraped of rust and barnacles and given a new coat of paint, he could make at least four knots more than when he had arrived. Thierichens hoped for a dark night with fog or thick weather with plenty of wind. When asked if he feared the half dozen British and French ships lying in wait off the Capes, he responded, "they may have more than us to fight."[30] According to one of his officers, German ships were also steaming off the coast. The *Eitel* gathered all the necessary provisions for departure, including essentials like water, tobacco and matches.[31] Thierichens even loaded "a large quantity of candy, including hundreds of decorated chocolate Easter eggs."[32] He closed off all entrances for visitors, and the crew began loading the more than 1,600 tons of coal that had been delivered to the *Eitel*. It was expected that the ship would be full of coal by morning.[33]

Later that day, the German crew was startled when a U.S. submarine pulled up alongside them. The sailors assumed it was British, as they had no idea a U.S. sub was nearby. The sub's crew exchanged greetings with the German sailors and then disappeared.[34] That same day, Washington delivered some official papers to Thierichens. He gave no comment as to their nature and said that he and his crew had to be very careful as to what information was released to the media, because there were British spies in the area. Anyone who came onboard had to have the appropriate clearance.[35]

The *Eitel*'s stay in Hampton Roads produced tension not only on the ship and harbor but also in the community. For example, when Colonel Ira A. Haynes, commander of Fort Monroe, boarded the *Alabama*, the guns on the ship fired a salute. When the shots rang out, residents of Old Point Comfort were surprised at the explosion and believed the battle had begun between German and Allied ships. The shots fired from the *Alabama* also alarmed the crew of the *Eitel*.[36] With heightened anxiety both on- and offshore, the ship took extra precautions during coaling. Sabotaging fuel was by far the easiest way for someone to destroy a ship, so more than two hundred men stood guard and inspected the coal to make certain that enemy agents did not slip explosives into the fuel. A local man tried to get near the *Eitel* and was stopped by several German sailors and then taken away by federal agents.[37] While the *Eitel*'s situation became more intense, Washington grew tired of delay and offered Thierichens one last chance to leave port.

On April 4, 1915, following reports of yet another British ship off the Virginia coast, Thierichens met with Rear Admiral James Meredith Helm, commandant of the Fourth Naval District, and Rear Admiral Frank Edmund Beatty, commandant of the Norfolk Navy Yard. All merchant ships were held up so that the *Eitel* could depart. Ships were kept in port until April 4, and it appeared that the United States was trying to get the *Eitel* out to sea. The *Virginian-Pilot and the Norfolk Landmark* claimed that "today's action by the U.S. is the first definite step taken to open the course to the sea to the *Prinz Eitel*."[38] The paper also pointed out the irony of the U.S. government helping the *Eitel* return to sea, because the German ship had sunk the American merchant ship *William P. Frye*.[39]

Captain Thierichens and Collector Hamilton had, since the raider arrived, been in correspondence regarding the amount of time needed for maintenance and reprovisioning of the *Eitel*, but after almost a month, Washington had had enough. The original letter from Hamilton to Thierichens explained that the "board of Naval officers found that it would take 14 days to repair the ship to its seaworthy condition."[40] Doing so would include fixing the boiler and gathering fuel and supplies. The board said that the *Eitel* would have until April 6 to complete repairs and fueling. The government set a date of April 7 for the Germans to leave or they would have to be interned.[41]

Collector Hamilton delivered the final ultimatum on April 7, 1915. He relayed the directions of his department: "I have to advise you that the *Prinz Eitel Friedrich*…must depart or otherwise be under the necessity of accepting internment within American jurisdiction during the continuance of the

Rear Admiral Frank Beatty served as commandant of the Norfolk Navy Yard from January 4 to November 25, 1915. *Naval History and Heritage Command.*

war in which your country is now engaged."[42] He requested that the *Eitel* depart U.S. waters by 4:00 a.m. on April 8, 1915. The government awaited Thierichens's response.

April 8 was a gloomy day for Captain Thierichens. The letter that he was about to submit would seal the fate of his ship and crew. He would be interned, stuck in the United States until the end of the war. The decision was not an easy one, but it had to be made. His letter was straightforward: "I inform you I intend to intern the SMS *Prinz Eitel Friedrich*."[43] He said that the main reason he did not leave was because the relief he expected never showed; without their help, the likelihood of an escape would be improbable due to the number of enemy cruisers.[44] "I have decided not to deliver my crew to almost certain destruction," lamented a melancholy Thierichens.[45] His last statement in the letter said that he would wait for orders from the United States.

Over the next few days, he responded to media questions as to why he didn't leave. Thierichens made a case for his crew's bravery and heroism. "I would like to have gone to sea myself," the German captain responded. "I would not hesitate to go, but I had to think of my men."[46] He described the scene: "You could have heard a pin drop.…Men had not tears: they are for women."[47] He defended the honor of his crew by saying, "Their love of the Fatherland is supreme and they are in deep mourning."[48] The sailors would have risked everything for their country to return to sea.

The last night they planned on going was Saturday. They received clearance from U.S. officials, and the captain wanted to go, but their boiler was not ready. The crew worked day and night, but they could never get the boiler right. Despite that problem and the lurking Allied ships, he continued to extol his bravery: "I would have gladly taken this ship out alone and taken the risk of getting by the enemies warships outside the entrance to the bay, but I had to think of…my crew."[49] His persistent defense that he would have gone out on his own despite the danger but for the consideration of his men shows that he may have never even considered leaving. He also wanted to make it clear as a German captain that he and his men were brave and that internment was not what they wanted but what they had to do. Thierichens regretted, "Now they will be idle."[50]

Secretary Daniels relayed orders and sent documents to Rear Admiral Beatty regarding the internment of the *Eitel*. Beatty communicated the provisions of internment based on President Wilson's proclamation of neutrality to Thierichens, and the German captain signed the document, making the terms official. One of the most important features of the commitment to internment is the promise that "captain should give pledge for himself, officers, and crew not to commit any unneutral act and not to leave limits prescribed in paroles."[51] Paroles involved the agreement between the German captain and the U.S. government that German sailors could move freely in the designated areas if they pledged that they would not do anything to violate neutrality. In addition to the parole, Washington ordered Thierichens to make the ship inoperable during internment. The sailors took down the armaments, disabled the radio and dismantled the propellers.[52]

Compounding the sadness that internment brought to the crew, one of their number was accidentally killed while working on the ship. Maximillian Furiar Berhard Prey died on April 7, 1915, when he fell from a ladder, rolled down a set of stairs and fractured his skull. He was the first German sailor killed since the ship left Tsingtao. The transferring of the *Eitel* from Newport News to the Norfolk Navy Yard in Portsmouth for internment was delayed so that the sailors could bury Prey. On April 9, both American and German sailors paid their respects to Prey at Greenlawn Memorial Park cemetery in Newport News with full military honors.[53] The ceremony was an indication of the relationship that was forming between the German sailors and the American government and military.

The internment of the *Eitel* was not the last German drama for the Hampton Roads community. Early on March 29, 1915, another German surface raider, the SMS *Kronprinz Wilhelm*, and its crew of 454 waited off the Virginia Capes, anticipating a sprint to neutral America to join the *Eitel*. With less than twenty-five tons of coal left in the ship and a crew sickened with beriberi, Kapitänleutnant Paul Wolfgang Thierfelder knew that his only choice was to steam past French and British ships to safety in Hampton Roads. The ship had been at sea for 251 days without seeing a port, and now it would attempt a dangerous mission to reach shore. His engineer, Lieutenant Brinkman, reported that the wireless told him that there were more than eight British cruisers in the area and that six of them were between the *Kronprinz* and the Virginia coast. They had to elude this British blockade in order to reach safety.[54] One of the officers aboard the German raider, Count Alfred von Niezychowski, described the obstacle as "a watchful cordon of battleships."[55] He also noted that they had "a plentiful number of outpost(s) in wireless touch with the blockading squadron."[56] The Allied ships were prepared for any blockade runners.

The *Kronprinz Wilhelm* was one of the largest luxury liners of the early twentieth century. The 25,000-ton, four-funneled passenger ship was converted into an armed surface raider when the war broke out. After a successful 251-day cruise, the ship ran low on fuel and supplies and sought refuge in Newport News. *U.S. Naval History and Heritage Command Photograph.*

Alfred von Niezychowski was from a Polish noble family. He was an officer aboard the *Viktoria Luise* when the war broke out, then he was transferred to the *Prinzess Irene* and then to the *Kronprinz Wilhelm*. His uncle was Baron Ladislaus Hengelmüller von Hengervár, formerly Austro-Hungarian ambassador at Washington. In 1928, Niezychowski published *The Cruise of the Kronprinz Wilhelm* about the adventures of the German raider and gave lectures on the raider's journey at sea. *University of Iowa Libraries.*

On April 10, the *Kronprinz* came within sixty miles of the Virginia coast. Thierfelder waited for darkness and then decided to make a sortie for the Capes. The intrepid captain called a meeting with his men. "There are six [British] cruisers outside the Capes," he said, "but with the help of God we will get through."[57] He called this action the most important moment during their eight-month voyage. If they could get within the three-mile limit of neutral waters, they would be safe.

When Count Niezychowski saw the Virginia coast, he wrote that it was "the first sign of shore I had seen in many a day, were so welcomed they seemed like home."[58] He believed that "behind those lights was a haven of safety, a great nation, friendly to both sides in the war, and now our sole hope of protection."[59] As they moved closer, they spotted two ships straight ahead about one mile apart from each other. They were British ships, and the *Kronprinz* had to go right between them. Thierfelder called to his engine room, "Lay on men! Now we're going through."[60] The ship inched closer and closer, hoping not to be spotted by the British. A few moments later, it made it within the three-mile limit. The crew was now in the neutral limits of U.S. waters. They had made it past the British cruisers; they were safe. The crew celebrated—"some danced," recalled Niezychowski, "some turned somersaults, and all acted as if possessed."[61] Niezychowski and other crew members knew that they could be interned and believed that "it sufficed that the ship was safe, had not been captured, had not been beaten on the sea."[62] The vessel that had destroyed fourteen merchant ships now sought refuge in a neutral harbor, the same port that held its sister ship, the *Prinz Eitel Friedrich*.

The next morning, April 11, 1915, as the *Kronprinz* neared the Virginia coast, an American ship came to its side and delivered two officers to pilot the German cruiser into the harbor. As the *Kronprinz*, now piloted by American officers, entered, American battleships rang out a salute, and the band aboard the *Kronprinz* played "Heil dir im Siegerkranz" ("Hail to Thee in Victor's Crown"), the German national anthem—ironically, played to the same tune as "My Country, 'Tis of Thee"). The band then continued with "The Star-Spangled Banner."[63]

The main complication for the German raider was not fuel and maintenance, but the sick crew. For the past few weeks, more than sixty members of the *Kronprinz* had been battling beriberi, a disease caused by a lack of vitamin B1 that could affect the nervous and cardiovascular systems.[64] The crew developed the disease from a lack of vegetables, as they had been at sea for more than two hundred days without adequately restocking.

Thierfelder knew that he must stall for time until his crew felt better. He was just as confident as Thierichens about his attempt to get back out to sea. "Just as easily and quietly as I slipped into this port I am going out," remarked the German captain. He made it clear that he did not want to stay. "I shall not ask to be interned," he insisted.[65] The next few weeks were similar to the time when the *Eitel* contemplated rushing back to sea, but many, including the American government and the German sailors, knew that their time was up and that they would spend the rest of the war in America.

The English, already frustrated by the *Eitel*'s arrival, were even more embarrassed to have another enemy ship slip through their blockade. Upset about their failure, they quickly pointed out instances where they thought the German ships had violated neutrality. One example was the sinking of the *Semantha*, a neutral Norwegian merchant ship. The British government claimed that the ship's grain cargo did not allow it to be sunk by the *Eitel* and that this should be considered by the U.S. government.[66] There were also accusations that the *Eitel* had used its wireless (which was supposed to be dismantled during internment) to help guide the *Kronprinz*. Both German captains denied the charges. When British officials complained of these violations, Captain Thierichens responded, "I have given my parole to the United States government, which is the word of honor of a man and German officer, and I think that should be enough. I have nothing further to say."[67]

Rationalizing the German cruiser's slip through the blockade, the British media reported that the *Kronprinz*'s entry into American waters was "a very satisfactory termination to her career as a raider of merchant shipping." The British papers stated that they didn't care if the raider was interned or not. If the vessel was not interned, then it would be destroyed by British ships. The internment of the two raiders meant that Britain did not have to worry about them terrorizing merchant shipping.

One of Thierfelder's goals, like Thierichens's, was to keep the enemy ships wondering about his next move. He believed the best way to fight the war onshore was to sow confusion among the Allies, causing them to keep ships patrolling off the Virginia Capes. The law was clear that the British cruisers must remain outside the three-mile limit, and the *Kronprinz*, like the *Eitel*, had to gain clearance from the U.S. government before it could leave. The British had an idea of what the *Kronprinz* was doing, and they reported in their papers that "a ship with 66 cases of beri-beri on board is a potential danger to the community; but the farce of pretending to fit out preparatory to making a dash for the open seas

Captain Paul Thierfelder became naval commander of the *Kronprinz* when Germany entered World War I. The quiet and confident captain was transferred from the SMS *Karlsruhe* with fifteen other men when Germany entered the war. *Norfolk Public Library, Norfolk, Virginia.*

terminated so ingloriously in the case of the *Eitel Friedrich* that the captain of the *Kronprinz Wilhelm* will have no encouragement from the people of Newport News, brag he never so loudly."[68] The paper also poked fun at the excitement surrounding the maritime community and the German captains by saying that "Americans love a little sensation, but Captain Thierichens overdid his part."[69]

As Thierfelder kept his ship in limbo in Hampton Roads, he met with Thierichens to discuss their next move. The captain, along with several of his officers, visited the *Kronprinz*. It's unclear what they talked about, but two topics that were probably discussed were American neutrality and the British blockade. The case of the *Odenwald* showed that they had to gain clearance before they left. One of the ship's officers, Lieutenant Albert Warnecke, called the case of the *Odenwald*, "the worst thing the Americans ever did to Germany."[70] The British ships would also be eager to make up for their failures of letting two of the enemy's ships into a U.S. port, and they did not want them to escape.

On April 12, 1915, U.S. officials came aboard the ship and inspected the *Kronprinz*. After reviewing the ship and finding that a major overhaul was necessary, Thierfelder requested three weeks to restore the raider to seaworthiness, after which they would leave. During this time, Dr. Joseph Goldberger of the U.S. Public Health Service found that ninety-four men now had beriberi. The port quarantine officer, Dr. Ward McCaffrey, believed that every sailor on the ship had the disease. The doctors requested fruit and vegetables to combat the disease and awaited the result.

The *Kronprinz* went into drydock at Newport News Shipbuilding & Dry Dock Company on April 14 for coaling and maintenance. The British continued to argue that the United States violated neutrality by helping the *Kronprinz* repair damage it had received during war. Thierfelder's plan was working. The German ship created delays and angered the British, so much so that some British sailors sent bomb-threat letters to Thierfelder and his crew. U.S. Marines were put on guard duty to ensure that no attempts to harm the ship were made.

The German raider had its bottom painted and restored on April 19; a few days later, new boiler tubes were added. Thierfelder requested the remaining supplies that he needed, then he waited. On April 26, he received instructions from the German government that they must be interned.

The *Kronprinz* and *Eitel* were tugged from Newport News to the Norfolk Navy Yard in Portsmouth, where they would spend the remainder of their internment in Virginia. *Portsmouth Naval Shipyard Museum.*

They had no chance of escaping past the British ships, and the German government implied that their escape was not a top priority.

The *Kronprinz* was officially interned on May 3, 1915. Daniels's letter to the naval officials in Hampton Roads gave instructions to transfer the *Kronprinz Wilhelm* to the navy yard for internment as soon as possible. He specified that the navy should follow the same procedure for internment that it followed for the *Eitel*. On May 4, 1915, Secretary Daniels sent Thierfelder the same document that he sent a month earlier to Thierichens. It described the president's neutrality proclamation, asking for a written pledge or parole accepting their conditions. Once the *Kronprinz* lay at anchor next to its sister ship in the Norfolk Navy Yard, the German sailors gave themselves up to go under the "protection and good will of the government of the United States."[71] These German sailors would remain in the country until the end of the war.

2

# THE CASE OF THE *WILLIAM P. FRYE* AND THE KAISER'S COURTEOUS PIRATES

O n November 6, 1914, the U.S. merchant ship *William P. Frye*, built in Bath, Massachusetts, and owned by Arthur Sewall and Company, left Seattle bound for England with a cargo of 5,036 tons of wheat. The *Frye*'s captain, H.H. Kiehne of Baltimore, made a relatively uneventful voyage until he was just off the Brazilian coast. Kiehne was surprised to discover that a German vessel was fast approaching. "I was almost becalmed when the German cruiser appeared about 2 o'clock in the afternoon of Jan. 27," he recalled.[72] Kiehne, on his first crossing as captain of the *Frye*, was caught off guard; he didn't even hear his officer yell "lay to."[73] It was too late to try to escape: the German commerce raider, the *Prinz Eitel Friedrich*, was now upon them.

Sailors from the *Eitel* boarded the ship and inspected the cargo. Captain Thierichens found the wheat aboard the *Frye*, said it was contraband and stated that he would destroy it. Despite Kiehne's protest that wheat was not a smuggled good, the German captain ordered the shipment thrown overboard. An officer and a small squad of men boarded the ship and helped the *Frye*'s crew throw the wheat into the sea.[74] Soon after the interception of the *Frye*, Thierichens's radio operator discovered that a French vessel, the *Jacobsen V. Leroux*, was only five miles away. Anticipating another potential prize, the *Eitel* left some of its men with the *Frye* to dispose of the wheat and went to investigate the *Jacobsen*. After safely transferring the twenty-four members of the French crew onto the German cruiser, the sailors destroyed the *Jacobsen* and returned to the *Frye* the next morning. Thierichens then removed the members of the *Frye*'s crew and put them on the raider. Once the Frye's crew was securely on the *Eitel*, the German sailors placed explosives in the vessel's hold and then set them off. Within an hour, the ship was sunk.[75] The *William P. Frye* was the first American vessel destroyed by German aggression during World War I.

Two months after the *Eitel* sank the *Frye*, the German cruiser, low on supplies and fuel, sought refuge in Hampton Roads. At that time, the U.S. government knew little about the *Frye* incident and reported that it would wait until receiving all of the details concerning the event before it passed judgment on the raider. It did, however, report that this was a serious situation—"on its face it [bore] the appearance of an unfriendly act on the part of a German ship of war, which must result in diplomatic negotiations with the German government."[76] As the *Eitel* entered U.S. territory, President Wilson requested that a full investigation be conducted.[77]

The *Eitel* intercepted the U.S. merchant ship *William P. Frye* on January 27, 1915, and sank the vessel the next day. *Library of Congress.*

President Woodrow Wilson launched a full investigation into the sinking of the *Frye. Library of Congress.*

American and German officials would argue over whether or not the *Eitel's* actions were justified for the next several years. The United States contested Thierichens's decision and said that wheat was not smuggled goods unless it was consigned to a belligerent or an agent of such government. The wheat was purchased by Heatley and Company of London, a private British company operating out of Seattle, and not an agent of the government.[78] The German government supported Thierichens's decision and argued that wheat was considered contraband, thus justifying the destruction of the *Frye.*

Once the United States entered World War I in 1917, the case was put on hold and not resolved until after the war. On October 30, 1925, American commissioner Chandler P. Anderson and German commissioner W. Kisselbach ruled that the German government pay an award of $91,450 to the ship's owner.[79] In 1926, the commissioners denied a request to cover further damages. They ruled that outside of the original award of $91,450, "the government of Germany is not obligated to pay to the government of the United States any further or additional amount on behalf of the claimants."[80] This judgment officially closed the case of the *William P. Frye.*[81]

While the governments tried to settle the case through diplomatic channels, Captain Thierichens had to deal with threats to his crew and ship, as they were staying in the country of one of their victims. As news of the *Frye* incident spread throughout the United States, some angered citizens tried to intimidate the German sailors. On March 18, 1915, Thierichens received a communication from Philadelphia to "beat it" out of the port or a bomb would be set off against his ship's hull.[82] Other letters called the sailors pirates. Thierichens responded by saying, "They are trying to spread negative and bitter feeling throughout the U.S. because of the *Frye.*"[83] He told reporters that even with these hostile notes there had been more letters in support of their situation.[84] Regardless of the outpouring of positive correspondence, this did not overshadow the danger, and Thierichens needed armed guards to safeguard the *Eitel* against any potential danger.[85] He defended his decision to sink the *Frye* while pointing to a copy of the London Declaration sitting on his desk.[86] The London Declaration concerning the Laws of Naval War was a set of rules for maritime law proposed in 1909. The declaration was signed by several nations—including Germany, the United States and the United Kingdom—but no nation had ever ratified the law. One of the sections addressed contraband, calling foodstuffs (wheat) "conditional contraband."[87]

As the story of the daring adventure of the *Eitel* and the sinking of the *Frye* reached Americans from coast to coast, some compared it to the cruise of the CSS *Alabama* during the Civil War. An Annapolis man sent the German captain a copy of the book on the *Alabama*'s episode.[88] He believed the story of Thierichens and the *Eitel* was similar to that of Confederate captain Raphael Semmes and the *Alabama*. Some people even equated the sinking of the *Frye* to the battle between the CSS *Alabama* and USS *Kearsage*. "It is certainly a flattering comparison," exclaimed Thierichens.[89] One of the major differences between the two vessels was their fate; the *Kearsage* sank the *Alabama* in battle, while the *Eitel* was interned.

The *Alabama* did have some similarities with the *Eitel*. Both were commerce raiders that preyed on ships carrying supplies, including wheat,

The CSS *Alabama* was a Confederate sloop of war that captured more than sixty Union vessels during the Civil War. The USS *Kearsage* sank the CSS *Alabama* on June 19, 1864. Some American citizens compared the *Eitel* to the *Alabama*. *Library of Congress.*

to the enemy. The *Eitel* sank eleven ships; the *Alabama* captured more than sixty prizes. The *Alabama* also had a much longer career, serving almost two years in the Confederate navy; the *Eitel* served for just under one year. The local community enjoyed making these comparisons between the two ships, but one group that did not give the *Eitel* any sympathy was the company that owned the *Frye*.[90]

Samuel S.W. Sewall, one of the partners of Sewall and Company, the owners of the ship, believed that the U.S. government should arrest Thierichens and his crew. The *Virginian-Pilot and the Norfolk Landmark* asserted that the *Frye* was a symbol of American shipping and that the Sewall family must be outraged at the sinking of the ship and its cargo.[91] W.J. Gauntlet, a representative of Sewall and Company, asked if the Navy Department had any objection to the presence of the *Eitel* in Hampton Roads. Daniels made it clear that the U.S. Navy did not oppose the German raider's being there and maintained that Thierichens would not be arrested.[92]

Gauntlet and the owner of the *Frye* were worried that the German raider could escape without giving them any compensation. According to the Navy Department, the ship was well guarded and was "docked almost within a stone's throw of the battleship *Pennsylvania*."[93] The *Frye*'s owner was outraged that the government allowed the *Eitel* to enter a U.S. port for repairs and fuel. Gauntlet called the sailors "pirates." "The Frye," he declared "carried a cargo that was marked 'non-contraband' by the Federal Insurance Bureau, and there was nothing but wheat aboard the ship."[94] They continued to be angered over the sinking of their merchant vessel and the fact that the United States allowed the German pirates to stay freely. In spite of Gauntlet's hostility toward Thierichens, Captain Kiehne and many of the *Frye*'s crew bore no ill will toward Thierichens.

Although Kiehne was Thierichens's prisoner, he and the German captain became good friends. Their cordial relationship began immediately after the *Eitel* intercepted the *Frye*. Both Kiehne and his wife, who was onboard, explained that they were treated very well from the beginning. When the German sailors sank the *Frye*, Mrs. Kiehne said that it caused a great pain in her heart to see her husband's vessel sent to the bottom, but the "officers and men of the *Prinz Eitel Friedrich* had shown them every consideration and that she had never seen kinder or more courteous people."[95] Despite the fact that they destroyed his ship, Kiehne agreed to help Thierichens and his crew reach safety in America.

Kiehne assisted the *Eitel's* efforts to sneak past Allied ships in order to get into Hampton Roads. He explained, "I told his [Thierichens's] officers I

Captain Kiehne of the *Frye* assisted Thierichens in guiding the German raider to safety in Hampton Roads. After Captain Kiehne and his wife were released, they came back to visit the German sailors and continued to have a positive relationship with the officers and crew. *Library of Congress.*

knew they were going to Newport News and where they could find a good shipyard."[96] As they got closer to the Virginia Capes, Thierichens asked Kiehne what he thought would be the best course of action to get to the Virginia port undetected.[97] Kiehne told the German captain to move north and then "strike due westerly into the coast."[98]

Thierichens followed Kiehne's recommendation, and the *Eitel* reached the Virginia coast without detection by Allied ships. There are two possible reasons why Kiehne assisted the *Eitel*: he wanted to protect his wife, children and crew from the Allied ships that were trying to sink the raider; or he wanted to help the German sailors safely get to shore. He most likely considered both reasons. Without Kiehne's guidance, the *Eitel* may have never made it to safety.[99]

The reason for Kiehne's help could also have stemmed from how well the *Frye*'s crew was treated by the German crew. They were given comfortable accommodations and seemed to bond with the German sailors. Captain Kiehne taught English to many of the German officers.[100] The cordial relationship between the crews continued once they arrived in Hampton Roads. On March 30, 1915, a short time after their release, Captain Kiehne, his wife and a group of ladies visited the *Eitel*. Captain Thierichens entertained his guests from the *Frye* and then returned all of their belongings to them. Kiehne continued to meet with Thierichens and his officers during their time of internment.

Despite the amiable feelings between these two dissimilar captains, rumors spread that when Thierichens seized the merchant ship he had

This image of Captain Kiehne's children illustrates the benevolence that the sailors showed toward the prisoners, especially children. *Library of Congress.*

personally lowered the *Frye*'s flag instead of allowing the ship's captain to do it himself. Thierichens responded, "I did not haul down the American flag on the *William P. Frye* as some papers have stated."[101] He was concerned with his image in the United States and didn't want people to think that their German visitors were intruders who didn't care about rules.[102] The accusation that they hauled down the vessel's flag greatly disturbed Thierichens. "No man on this ship touched the American flag," he protested.[103] He explained that Captain Kiehne was the one who took down the flag. He brought it on the *Eitel,* and Mrs. Kiehne kept it for the remainder of the voyage.[104]

The *Virginian-Pilot and the Norfolk Landmark* illustrated the irony of the cordial relationship between captor and victim in a cartoon. Captain Kiehne and the crew of the *Frye* are shown in a rowboat watching the *Eitel* destroy their ship. The next picture portrays the crew of the *Frye* on the Virginia shore, wishing the *Eitel* good luck as it disembarks. The sketch presents the *Eitel* ready to sail, with British cruisers off in the distance. The text reads: "The captain and crew of the William P. Frye, which was sunk

THE CAPTAIN AND CREW OF THE WILLIAM P. FRYE, WHICH—

[Copyright: 1915: By John T. McCutcheon.]

—was sunk by the Prinz Eitel **Friedrich**, will—

—be down to see the Prinz Eitel off when it leaves **Newport News** for the open sea.

This cartoon in the *Virginian-Pilot and Norfolk Landmark* of March 18, 1915, shows the goodwill between the crew of the *Frye* and the crew of the *Eitel*. *Norfolk Public Library, Norfolk, Virginia.*

by the *Prinz Eitel Friedrich*, will be down to see the *Prinz Eitel* off when it leaves Newport News for the open sea."[105]

Regardless of Captain Kiehne's help and generosity, the opinions of the crew of the *Frye* were mixed. Several members of the *Frye's* crew did not care as much about being captured as they did about getting paid. They had not received any wages during their forty-three days aboard the *Eitel*

45

and now believed that the German government owed them compensation. However, the lack of payment did not harm the relationship between the crews of the *Eitel* and the *Frye*. On March 12, 1915, the crew of the *Frye* demonstrated that they held no ill feelings toward their captors by "sending, with their compliments to the German cruiser eight kegs of beer for the crew and cigars for the officers."[106] This gesture confirmed the goodwill and camaraderie between the two groups. Other crews captured by the *Eitel* were not as sympathetic.

Captain J.W. King of the British ship *Inverncoe* said his men were given time to collect their belongings before the Germans sank the ship.[107] However, Captain Mouission of the French ship *Florida* said that the crew of the *Eitel* appeared to be generous at first, but that, once they boarded the ship, they took all the food and did not share with any of the *Florida's* crew.[108] Mouisson also recalled that "the *Eitel Friedrich*…flew no flag when approaching a vessel and that the vessels captured had no way of telling the nationality of the Germans."[109]

Captain Wedgewood of the British steamer *Willerby* tried to ram the German cruiser when the *Eitel* began to intercept his vessel. "I thought it would be better to take our own boats at sea, than to be taken on board by the German," explained Wedgewood.[110] His attempt failed, and Thierichens sent an officer to the *Willerby* and requested that he take down his flag. "I refused," said Wedgewood. Thierichens hauled down the flag and told Wedgewood, "You're my prisoner and your ship is a prize of war."[111] They took the crew of the *Willerby* off the vessel, loaded them onto the German raider and sent the British ship to the bottom.[112]

Complaints from other captains concerned food and accommodations. When the *Eitel's* crew took two pigs from the British sailing ship *Mary Ada Short*, Captain Dobbin complained about not getting any share of the meat. Dobbin and Wedgewood also complained about their accommodations; they were berthed in the front compartment, while the *Frye's* crew was in the more comfortable rear quarters.[113]

The sinking of the *Frye* could have had a detrimental effect on the relationship between the United States and Germany. Shortly after the *Eitel's* internment, the local paper grouped the sinking of the *Frye* in the same list of naval attacks as the sinking of the *Lusitania*. On May 7, 1915, a German sub sent the Cunard passenger ship to the bottom of the ocean. More than one thousand people perished, including more than one hundred Americans. The incident sparked major outrage throughout England and the United States. According to the local paper, "The sinking

The Cunard ocean liner RMS *Lusitania* left New York bound for Liverpool, but it never made it. The ship was sunk on May 7, 1915, off the southern coast of Ireland by a German U-boat. More than 1,000 passengers died, including 128 Americans. *Library of Congress.*

of the American steamer, *Frye*…and the torpedoing of the giant liner *Lusitania* constitute a series of some incidents which the president is trying to interpret."[114]

Despite the case of the *Frye* and potential threats to neutrality, the German sailors were not seen as villains but as members of the Hampton Roads community, where they would live comfortably for eighteen months. The crew of the *Frye* considered the sailors not barbarians, but "courteous pirates," and these feelings would be echoed by local businesses, churches and residents throughout Hampton Roads.

# 3

# GERMAN SAILORS IN HAMPTON ROADS

## TOURISM, BEER AND THE TINY VILLAGE

Many merchants and local officials in Hampton Roads viewed the German raiders' internment as an economic benefit. The sailors purchased goods from stores, ranging from food and beer to shoes and musical instruments. They visited doctors, dentists and hospitals, and the presence of their unfamiliar ships and the tiny village that they built created a major tourist destination in the maritime community.

The economic advantage of having a large number of foreign sailors in the region began even before internment. Shortly after the *Eitel* anchored, Captain Thierichens granted leave to several hundred of his men. On April 3, 1915, they left Newport News and ventured into Norfolk to explore the maritime community and purchase goods. Some even attended a motion picture show.[115] On April 14, soon after the *Kronprinz* arrived, Captain Thierfelder sent his paymaster into Norfolk with $1,000 in German gold. He went to the bank and converted it into small change in order to settle fuel and repair accounts that the vessel had accrued since it had docked.[116] A week later, Thierfielder also purchased a new boiler for the *Kronprinz* and had it installed in the shipyard at Newport News.[117]

Once the *Eitel* and *Kronprinz* were interned, Captain Thierichens arranged for F. Besmer, a crew member of the *Kronprinz*, and Charles Marks, a resident of Norfolk, to do all of the shopping for the crews. U.S. naval officials questioned Marks's citizenship status, and the German captain responded that "he never belonged to one of our crews."[118] He explained that Marks met with Rear Admiral Beatty and that the commandant had given him

As soon as the sailors entered Newport News, they received permission to venture into the surrounding region. They had been at sea for more than two hundred days and were desperately in need of rest and relaxation. *Virginia Historical Society (2008.62.1).*

permission to buy goods for the crews of both raiders. Marks helped with purchasing everything from sheet music for the band, Christmas supplies, sporting goods and cooking supplies, to the bimonthly shipment of kegs of Pabst Blue Ribbon beer from the regional Norfolk distributor.

Hampton Roads benefited not only from the sailors as consumers but also from the tourism they generated. Local boating companies took advantage of the novelty of these foreigners and offered sightseeing tours of the vessels even before they were interned. Only a few days after the *Eitel* arrived, an announcement in the *Virginian-Pilot* read, "The steamer *Clio* of Norfolk Virginia Steamboat Company will make a special trip to Newport News to view the German *Prinz Eitel Friedrich*."[119] The paper reported on the spectacle: "curious folk flocked here today to view the German cruiser."[120] Since the *Eitel* had not yet been interned, extra security precautions were taken to ensure safety for both the tourists and the sailors; the "visitors were not permitted to board the ship, but hundreds…gazed at her as she lay at her dock."[121]

Interest in the German raiders was far greater than for U.S. Navy vessels. On March 21, 1915, big letters at the bottom of the *Virginian-Pilot*

Local boating companies took full advantage of the presence of the German ships and sailors. Newspaper advertisements listed the curious German raiders as a once-in-a-lifetime opportunity. The German sailors appeared happy to show off their mascots and other prizes they had acquired while at sea. *Library of Congress.*

exclaimed, "See the German cruiser *Prinz Eitel Friedrich* today and also the U.S.S. *Pennsylvania* just launched."[122] The German raider was listed as the main attraction, while the new U.S. battleship was treated as a secondary one. The tourist boat left from the wharf at Commerce Street and cost fifty cents for adults and twenty-five cents for children under twelve. The tour company expected a large response, "no crowding, only limited number of tickets sold."[123] Boating excursion companies continued to earn money from the German ships, even as tensions heightened because of the *Eitel*'s threat to depart.

On March 28, 1915, the same week the *Virginian-Pilot* described Hampton Roads as a "warlike scene," the paper announced a sightseeing daytrip aboard the steamship *Endeavor* to see the *Eitel*. After gaining special clearance, the boat planned to dock near the Newport News Shipbuilding & Dry Dock Company so that passengers could have an unobstructed view of the German cruiser.[124] This was an "opportunity which has not been given—make use of it."[125] Bad weather couldn't stop the program; the boating outing would proceed rain or shine.[126]

The USS *Pennsylvania*, built by the Newport News Shipbuilding & Dry Dock Company, was launched on March 16, 1915. *Norfolk Public Library, Norfolk, Virginia.*

*Above*: Some of the crew members of the *Eitel* loved receiving the attention of the steamboat touring companies, and many of them posed for pictures. *Library of Congress.*

*Opposite*: The Dewey Day Carnival was named after Admiral George Dewey, one of the most famous U.S. naval officers and the only officer to hold the rank of admiral of the navy. The carnival included all sorts of entertainment, but the main attraction was a chance to see German sailors and to go aboard the merchant raiders. *Norfolk Public Library, Norfolk, Virginia.*

On April 25, 1915, the *Virginian-Pilot* indicated that the steamer *Endeavor* would make one more outing to see the *Kronprinz*. It was a perfect opportunity, the paper claimed, because the ship was still lying "in stream" in Newport News. The advertisement promised that the tourists would be within speaking distance of the cruiser and urged readers to bring their cameras to capture this once-in-a-lifetime opportunity.[127] Boating companies were not the only entities capitalizing on the presence of the *Eitel* and *Kronprinz*.

The Norfolk Chamber of Commerce knew that these foreign vessels drew large crowds and used them for their benefit as well. The newspaper ranked the *Eitel* as one of the main attractions at the annual Dewey Day Carnival. The cruiser was listed alongside snake eaters, athletic events and circus performances, reported the local paper.[128] Visitors would be allowed on the ship if they gained the proper authorization from German and American

The Kirn building in Norfolk, Virginia, was named after Henry Kirn Jr.'s father. Henry Kirn Jr. became good friends with Thierichens. His father immigrated to the United States in the 1850s from Württemberg, Germany, eventually settled in Norfolk and became a prominent businessman. *Norfolk Public Library, Norfolk, Virginia.*

Opened in 1898, the Monticello Hotel was one of the best hotels in Norfolk, located on City Hall Avenue and Granby Street. Theirichens was invited to a business meeting there with government officials and other prominent citizens to discuss improvements to the Norfolk Navy Yard. *Norfolk Public Library, Norfolk, Virginia.*

Corporations and business conferences added the German ships to their itinerary. *Portsmouth Naval Shipyard Museum.*

representatives.[129] The festival will contain "a wide variety of attractions so many in fact that the visitor will be puzzled as to which ones to take in," claimed the paper.[130] The paper listed the wide range of attractions: "Submarine maneuvers, the old frigate *Constellation*, the *Prinz Eitel Friedrich* battleship, sham battles, drills and countless other attractions have been arranged, and the ball on the USS *Richmond* promise to be of unusual brilliance."[131]

The chamber used the German ships to market the navy yard as an ideal location for corporate gatherings and meetings. On June 10, 1915, the *Virginian-Pilot* headlines boasted, "Businessmen will view new waterfront, second outing of association will include warehouses and interned German cruisers."[132] More than 150 businesses in the area received invitations. The solicitation included a description of the waterfront inspection and a notice that the visitors will have a chance to observe an inspection of the *Eitel* and *Kronprinz*.[133]

Regular visitors to the ship included prominent members of the community and top city and state officials. On April 2, 1915, a group of men boarded the *Eitel*: U.S. senator Thomas Martin; Virginia state senator

Goodrich Hatton; Elliot Milstead, a member of the Virginia House of Delegates; George McBain, principal of Maury High School; Henry Kirn Jr., a local businessman; and the mayor of Norfolk, Wyndham R. Mayo.[134] Captain Thierichens greatly enjoyed the company of Kirn, whose father was a native of Germany and wished to see him back in their home country. However, Thierichens was tired of all of the social gatherings and big events, and he longed for a nice, quiet evening. "When I come back I will be glad to go to your home and dine," he said to Kirn, "and when I come, let's not have any banquet and crowds—just you and I and some noodles soup."[135]

On April 13, Captain Thierichens entertained Congressman Homer P. Snyder of the Thirty-Third Congressional District of New York on his ship, and the congressman reciprocated the favor by hosting the captain, Collector of Customs Hamilton, and several well-known businessmen the next day at the Monticello Hotel.[136] The businessmen discussed the importance of the Norfolk Navy Yard to economic interests throughout the country. Congressman Snyder's interest in the navy yard may have come from his manufacturing background in textiles and vehicles. Thierichens told them that the hospitality and quality of the harbor was top-notch. "You have such a magnificent harbor here," explained the German captain.[137] Snyder said that he would go back to Congress and "push for the improvement of both the local harbor and...the betterment of the Norfolk Navy Yard."[138]

A few days after the *Kronprinz*'s arrival, the ship welcomed additional important guests, including Major Russell Benjamin Harrison. The son of President Benjamin Harrison had served in the Spanish-American War as consul to Mexico. He was stopping by Hampton Roads on business and was interested in viewing the German cruisers on April 27. The paper reported that "they were all cordially received by Commander Thierfelder and the crew told the stories of the sea raider."[139] Several of the guests were from Petersburg, Virginia, and offered invitations to the captain and his officers to visit their town. The captain responded that, if interned, they would almost certainly go there, and his guests were "confident that several of the daring sailors will visit Petersburg."[140] Once interned, the interest in the ships as a tourist attraction grew.

On May 6, Captain Thierfelder invited several special guests to celebrate the thirty-third birthday of Crown Prince Friedrich Wilhelm Victor August Ernst, for whom their ship was named. The crew hung an autographed portrait of the crown prince, eldest son of Kaiser Wilhelm II. Visiting hours were extended, and the crew decorated the salon and outfitted the *Kronprinz* for a large party. Thierfelder sent special invitations to the mayors of Portsmouth and Norfolk and the governor and former governor of South Dakota.[141] The birthday party also served as a fundraiser for the families of German sailors and soldiers.[142]

General visitors also had the opportunity to tour the *Eitel*. On a tour through the ship, guests could buy a beer and a sandwich in the Ratskeller for less than five cents. There were also cafés in the navy yard that sold nonalcoholic beverages. The purchase and sale of alcohol aboard the vessel would create some problems with local congregations.

Reverend J.L. Westfall of South Street Baptist Church in Norfolk visited the German raider on May 23, 1915, and observed the sale of alcohol to several American citizens. He then formed a committee with other preachers in the area to draft a letter to Secretary Daniels concerning the illegal sale of beer on the foreign cruiser on Sunday. Westfall reported to the group that during his time on the cruiser he "tasted the beverage to satisfy himself it was beer."[143] The minister and his party purchased six rounds total (!) and reported that there were "100 persons about him."[144] He preached to his congregation the next Sunday against alcohol abuse and the sale of alcohol on Sunday. (The sale of alcohol on Sunday was illegal in Virginia. Secretary of the Navy Daniels had outlawed alcohol on navy ships in 1914.) The preacher involved the local police, but they could do little, because the beverage was sold on a foreign ship. As a compromise, the German captains agreed not to sell beer to visitors on Sunday.

The United States had debated relocating the ships to Philadelphia since their arrival. The main reason to move them was to make room for the expansion of the Norfolk Navy Yard. If they were ever moved to another city, it would be a major blow to the Hampton Roads economy. When Mayor Mayo and the president of the Norfolk Chamber of Commerce, Barton Myers, heard rumors that the *Eitel* and *Kronprinz* might move to Philadelphia, they left for Washington immediately to meet with Secretary Daniels to convince him to keep the ships in Hampton Roads.

One of the main arguments against transferring the raiders to Philadelphia was the potential engagement with British and French vessels en route. When asked about the possibility of moving the ships, Mayor Mayo said that "it is understood…that the place for final internment…was brought up and Secretary Daniels is expected to make a final decision while here today." Norfolk and Portsmouth officials conferred with Daniels on April 30, 1915, about the situation and argued that there was more than enough

The sailors became so popular that they needed to put restrictions on their guest passes so that their ships did not become overcrowded. *Hampton Roads Naval Museum.*

space for them, and if they relocated the cruisers to another port it "will be a heavy blow."[145] On May 1, Daniels made the decision to keep them at the Norfolk Navy Yard until the end of the war. (They would actually be moved to Philadelphia in September 1916 to make room for the expansion of the Norfolk Navy Yard.) He explained that the chamber of commerce, board of trade and other business groups protested to keep the ships in Hampton Roads.[146] Because of the potential for disaster from towing the German vessels past Allied warships to Philadelphia and the outrage from Norfolk and Portsmouth government officials and merchants, the *Eitel* and *Kronprinz* would remain in Hampton Roads indefinitely.

By June 1915, the German sailors became so popular that Thierichens and Thierfelder set up strict visiting hours to control the crowds. Despite their concerns, the captains still had requests for groups to go aboard their vessels. For example, U.S. representative Edward Everett Holland of Suffolk, Virginia, wrote to Rear Admiral Beatty and asked permission for Dr. H.W. Campbell and his friends to tour the raiders. Holland explained that "Dr. Campbell is one of our best citizens, a man of excellent character and habits, and I know will give you no trouble, if granted this permission."[147] Holland was aware of the restrictions, but

A large vacant space that would eventually be used for the expansion of the Norfolk Navy Yard was reserved for the sailors. It took almost six months for them to build the tiny German Village. *Norfolk Public Library, Norfolk, Virginia.*

he replied that "if permission can be secured for him, I shall very much appreciate it."[148]

Even though they shortened the hours of visitation, overcrowding was still an issue for Thierichens and his men. He described his unease over pass control in a letter to Beatty. "I understand that such allowances were given in order to enable us to control the visitor by ourselves," explained the German captain.[149] The constraints were placed so that both the navy yard and the interned ships were not exceeding capacity, especially concerning unwanted guests. His main complaint was that the sentries who were posted to guard the sailors had too much control over the passes. They would use their own discretion on who was allowed or denied access. The sentries did not follow the list of authorized individuals who had been given clearance. Beatty ordered the sentries to permit visitors with the appropriate paperwork, which appeased Thierichens, but arguments over permits continued throughout their stay.[150]

The ships were popular tourist destinations, but the main attraction was the German Village that the sailors built, named "Eitel Wilhelm" after the two raiders. In the fall of 1915, after Rear Admiral Walter McLean (who took over as commandant in November 1915) allowed the Germans to use an area at the navy yard reserved for the expansion of the facility, the crews began creating the village out of scraps of glass, lumber and other materials. It eventually included more than fifty colorfully painted miniature buildings. The idea came from Officer Graf of the *Eitel*. He believed that if they built their own village, they could occupy their time through other means than marching and drilling. He also wished to re-create their own German town, since they would be in the United States until the war ended. Graf's idea came to life after almost six months of hard labor, and when it was completed it became one of the major tourist destinations on the East Coast.[151]

The quaint structures included a church, newspaper office, telegraph station, postmaster station, fire department, police station, gymnasium, bowling alleys, marriage license bureau and several other little German villas. The cottages were decorated with "sunflower and hollyhock gardens, red roofs, white curtains and carvings along the eaves and fenceposts."[152] They were named after German ships, including *Emden*, *Karlsruhe* and *Luchs*. Captain Thierichens had commanded the *Luchs*, and Captain Thierfelder had served as a navigating officer aboard the *Karlsruhe*.

More than one thousand people toured the small replica village one day in 1916.[153] Tourists flocked to experience German culture and craftsmanship. The visitors walked through the streets labeled with German names and viewed the many attractions. The sailors charged ten cents for entry. They performed acrobatic shows, sang songs and gave concerts. One guest remarked on the spectacle of the community, calling it "an atmosphere of "Kaiser, and Kultur, and Wiener Schnitzel and good sturdy Lutheranism…and everything one could find in an honest, hard working German town of the old country."[154] The sailors could not go home, so they built their home at the Norfolk Navy Yard.

The village was not only for tourists. The main reason it was built was to create a sense of the Fatherland for *Eitel*'s and *Kronprinz*'s crews, who were interned in a foreign country until the end of the war. They built their own parks equipped with tiny lakes and gardens. To continue their sense of German patriotism, they planted flowers in the rose garden to form a shape similar to an iron cross. The garden provided a source of cucumbers, tomatoes, radishes and other vegetables. Their farm also included some of the animals that they had acquired on their voyage to the Virginia shores, along with new ones that they purchased while staying in Hampton Roads.

One of the only signs in English was located on the road next to the farm: "WARNING! GO SLOW! BE CAREFUL OF CHICKEN, PIGEONS AND DUCKS."[155] These

*This page*: The village featured more than fifty miniature structures, gardens, street signs and everything one could find in a town in the old country. *Portsmouth Naval Shipyard Museum.*

Tourists flocked to see the spectacle of the German Village. Sailors sold postcards, the *Kolonie-Anzeiger* and trinkets to benefit the German Red Cross. *Portsmouth Naval Shipyard Museum.*

*Above and opposite*: Some of the structures in the village included a fire station, a post office, a marriage license bureau, a church and other buildings that helped form a sense of community for the sailors. *Portsmouth Naval Shipyard Museum.*

*This page*: The village was home to several dogs, chickens, goats, ducks and pigs. The sailors had acquired many of the animals from their journey at sea. *Library of Congress.*

The village included several vegetable and flower gardens. The vegetable gardens were a source of food for sailors, and the flower gardens were used to decorate the village. *Portsmouth Naval Shipyard Museum.*

agriculture areas provided sources of food and created a homelike atmosphere, but they could not replicate home life exactly.

When asked about the village, the owner of one of the villas explained, "not all perfect, *nein.*"[156] "*Wo-wo-wo-*where is *die Mutter*? Where is Gretchen?" he asked.[157] Their new home lacked a woman; a mother, a wife and a daughter. They could try to recreate the Fatherland structurally, but they could not recreate their households. Since they could not see their loved ones, the sailors thought of ways to help the women and children back home. All entry fees to the village were donated to the German Red Cross to help the families of soldiers and sailors. They found other ways to make money for the charity, including selling souvenirs, postcards, children's toys and their paper, the *Kolonie-Anzeiger.*

The sailors became a major tourist destination, and the residents of Hampton Roads welcomed them as part of their community. They also participated in activities alongside locals in church services, baseball games and other social activities that made them even more of a part of American society.

# 4

# THE ACTIVITIES OF INTERNED SAILORS

## BASEBALL, RELIGION AND PARTIES

During their internment, the sailors found leisure pursuits and other activities to pass the time, many of them part of American culture. The crew members observed sporting and military demonstrations and participated in religious services alongside local citizens. They celebrated holidays together and even continued their own traditions by interacting with other German crews who anchored in U.S. port cities. The sailors also participated in recreation and boating exercises within the prescribed limits of the navy yard.

The confinement of the *Eitel* and *Kronprinz* in one of the largest ports in the United States allowed the German sailors to witness a variety of military demonstrations. Rear Admiral Beatty asked Captain Thierichens to participate in the Fourth of July ceremonies in 1915. The German captain, delighted at the chance to join in America's birthday celebration, happily agreed to dress the ships for the festivities.[158] Later that month, on July 15, they viewed naval exercises at Fort Monroe, including target practice. The *Virginian-Pilot and the Norfolk Landmark* highlighted the event: "Last night gunners from Fortress Monroe opened fire on targets that illuminated the sky."[159] The firing began at 10:00 p.m., and the spectators at Ocean View included German sailors and local citizens. The two groups mingled while observing the spectacle. The colorful green shells from the fort illuminated the sky as the projectiles headed toward their targets pulled by tugs five miles offshore.[160] Military demonstrations were only one of the many experiences shared between the German sailors and the community.

Fort Monroe (or Fortress Monroe) was completed in 1834. Its strategic location along coastal Virginia has earned it the nickname "Gibraltar of the Chesapeake Bay." *Norfolk Public Library, Norfolk, Virginia.*

The crews of the *Eitel* and *Kronprinz* were introduced to America's leading pastime, baseball. They went to games and even began playing the sport in the navy yard. On April 23, 1915, several of the German sailors went into Portsmouth to attend the opening day of the Virginia (Baseball) League. The game, featuring Norfolk and Portsmouth, was a pitcher's duel that ended with Norfolk winning, 2–0. The president of the Virginia League, J.O. Boatwright, threw out the first pitch and greeted the sailors following the game.[161]

Thierichens requested permission for the men to go ashore to view another baseball game in Portsmouth on the afternoon of July 10. Rear Admiral Beatty, commandant of the Norfolk Navy Yard, allowed the men to go under Officer Niezychowski's watch, but they had to be kept "in formation, and must return immediately at the end of the game."[162] Even though the sailors regularly entered the cities of Norfolk and Portsmouth, they were still not free. Any time large numbers traveled off the navy yard, Washington required they be escorted by armed guards and kept in a tight formation to prevent any chance of a mass escape. The commandants hoped the sailors would embrace the game and encouraged them to practice in the navy yard.

After watching the contest, the sailors created a baseball field and began playing the game themselves. McLean not only allowed the men to use the field; he also extended the hours for use during the summertime. The ability to exercise during the cooler times provided a more comfortable and enjoyable experience.[163] On May 10, 1916, McLean changed the hours to between 6:00 a.m. and sunset for baseball and other sports but made it clear that this was not simply time for socializing: "smoking will be prohibited there, and the field should not be considered a general lounging place."[164] McLean explained that the purpose of the new hours and the boundary limits is "to give your [Thierichens's] men opportunity to indulge in games for which the present assigned limits do not afford space."[165]

After learning the game and playing it, the sailors hoped to bring this highlight of popular American culture back to the Fatherland. Their participation in one of the great American experiences, the national pastime, baseball, indicated that these foreigners were accepted and even encouraged to take part in American sporting events. This signified that the local community wanted to bond with the crew members and expose them to elements of their culture. By building the baseball field in their confined area, the sailors revealed that they were interested in becoming a part of American society.

The sailors also wished to participate in religious observances, even though there were few local services in their native language. They went to mass and

Rear Admirals Beatty and McLean gave the sailors a large amount of space in the navy yard for sporting activities. *Portsmouth Naval Shipyard Museum.*

holiday programs at churches in Norfolk and Portsmouth. On May 3, 1915, more than five hundred people attended Sunday school at Monumental Methodist Church in Portsmouth, including crew members of the *Eitel* and *Kronprinz*. The paper reported that "it was the largest number of the year that received the Holy Communion."[166] They regularly participated in the Eucharist at St. Paul's Catholic Church in Portsmouth. The parish, formed in 1804, was originally heavily attended by Irish and English immigrants. By the end of the nineteenth century, the church saw an increase in German and Italian attendees. Taking part in church services with local residents showed the benevolence between the interned sailors and Hampton Roads community. They were welcome to take part alongside American residents and U.S. sailors (who were stationed in Hampton Roads) in sacred religious services. These experiences were made possible through the close quarters and experiences of the internment situation.

The sailors' winter holiday activities for 1915 included Christmas mass, dinners and parties. On December 3, Thierichens sent a letter to McLean requesting permission for Chief Engineer Muller to go onshore to discuss Christmas service with a clergyman from St. Paul's.[167] The two met to discuss the service, and later that week Secretary of the Navy Daniels granted the sailors leave to go ashore to celebrate the holy day. On December 25, "255 sailors marched from the yard to the church accompanied by United States escorts."[168] They sat in pews alongside U.S. sailors from the Norfolk Navy Yard and the navy yard annex at St. Helena while Reverend E.A. Brodmann, chaplain of the battleship USS *New Hampshire* delivered the sermon. When mass concluded, the U.S. military escorted the interned sailors out of the church and back to the navy yard.[169] The holiday season continued for the crews of the *Eitel* and *Kronprinz* as they decorated their ships in Christmas greenery, as were all of the other battleships and vessels in the navy yard.[170]

On December 26, Thierichens made an additional request to have their own holiday party. The sailors wished to go to the Cape Charles Ferry Boat and pick up eleven ladies arriving from New York for the party. McLean granted them permission to make as many trips as they needed from 7:30 a.m. to 3:00 p.m.[171] Less than a week later, they hosted a New Year's Eve party. The event was well attended, and even the famous *Baltimore Sun* newspaper editor H.L. Mencken attended the festivities. Mencken had become acquainted with Thierfelder, Thierichens, Niezychowski and other officers of the *Eitel* and *Kronprinz* when they came to Baltimore to see some of the German reservists and crews of the German merchant ships who were interned there. At their visit, Mencken noted that "though their ships

Located at the intersection of Washington and High Streets in downtown Portsmouth, St. Paul's Catholic Church was a regular place of worship for the German sailors. *Norfolk Public Library, Norfolk, Virginia.*

Celebrated writer H.L. Mencken (*left*) was an admirer of German culture. While editor of the *Baltimore Sun*, he met some of the German sailors near his home and attended their New Year's Eve party aboard the *Eitel* in 1915. His interest in the German sailors may have stemmed from the fact that his grandfather was born in Germany. *Theatre Magazine*.

Eugen Perrenon's grave at the Captain Theodore H. Conaway Memorial Naval Cemetery in Portsmouth, Virginia. Dr. Perrenon passed away in November 1915, and the U.S. Navy allowed the interned sailors to participate in a full military funeral, including the firing of a volley over the grave. *Author's collection*.

were interned, they had a considerable freedom of movement."[172] He greatly enjoyed the New Year's Eve party aboard the interned cruisers. He recalled a few important moments during the evening. One was that Elsie, McLean's wife, was pregnant, and "Thierichens...offered a toast to her and the newcomer, greatly to her delight."[173] The second was that Niezychowski had to cut off the beer supply, because he believed the men had a lower tolerance for alcohol than the navy sailors aboard. Mencken may have overindulged, because on his return trip the next morning, he recalled, "I was so much used up that I slept all the way."[174] The presence of the renowned editor showed that the interned Germans were of interest beyond just the Hampton Roads community. The sailors' holiday party was another example of the close bond among U.S. citizens, naval officials and the interned sailors. There was a great deal of trust and camaraderie at these parties where Americans and Germans ate and drank together.

The crews of the *Eitel* and *Kronprinz* also participated in the Portsmouth Christmas celebration in 1916. On December 20, Thierichens wrote to McLean asking for approval to "send 4 officers, 2 warrant officers and 156 petty officers and men to St. Paul's church in Portsmouth for divine service on 25th of December." Thierichens explained that they would like to leave around 9:15 a.m. and take a shortcut to avoid the extra time it would take to go all the way around the navy yard.[175] McLean responded on December 21 and granted permission for the party to go ashore, but he ordered the sailors to return immediately after the service.[176] This exchange of correspondence shows that men of the *Eitel* and the *Kronprinz* were allowed to interact with the local community, but they were not free; they still had to follow orders and could not loiter in the city or stay overnight. They had to return to the navy yard. Participation in holiday celebrations was another social activity that linked the sailors and the local population. Intimate meals, parties and religious observances clearly indicated that the presence of 800 German sailors in the Virginia maritime community was a unique and special situation. Hampton Roads' Christian population was not the only religious group to embrace the sailors. Other denominations were very open and willing to allow the Germans to participate in their religious activities.

Norfolk's Jewish community invited sailors to their synagogue. On September 5, 1915, the *Virginian-Pilot and the Norfolk Landmark* advertised, "Hebrew Sailors Invited to Attend Local Services."[177] The president of the Ahavath Israel Congregation, N. Cohen, sent several letters to the German captains asking if any of their men wished to join the congregation. In one letter to Thierichens, Cohen asked Thierfelder and Thierichens "to permit the men of your ship of the Hebrew faith to attend the most sacred service… which occurs on Thursday and Friday, September 9 and 10 and then again on the Saturday following, September 18."[178] He told Thierichens that he would be grateful if he allows his sailors to attend. "This is one holiday which we believe is observed by almost every Hebrew in the world," explained Cohen.[179] He did not want them to be left out and assured them that it would be in their best interest to participate. He also commended Thierichens for his cooperation in giving his men an option to join in the ceremonies.[180] He continued to try to accommodate the sailors by making it clear that the congregation will "set aside a certain part of our synagogue where your men will be given every courtesy possible."[181] Cohen extolled the importance of the religious holiday and offered to arrange lodgings for the men if they needed to stay over.[182] It's unclear if the sailors took part in the festivities that Cohen offered, but this illustrated the bonds between the foreign sailors and the local community. Religious leaders went out of their way to involve the interned sailors in their religious observations.

Along with holy services, the men of the *Eitel* and *Kronprinz* conducted funeral ceremonies for crew members who died while interned. On November 4, 1915, after the death of Dr. Eugen Perrenon of the *Kronprinz*, Thierichens sent Rear Admiral Beatty an attendance list and requested rifles and ammunition so they could fire a volley over the grave. The next day, Beatty approved the attendance list and ordered guns and ammunition to be delivered to Thierichens before the funeral. The captain invited Beatty to attend, but the American officer declined "due to some most important urgent work required by the Navy Department."[183] Beatty thanked Thierichens and Thierfelder for the invitation and regretted that work had prevented him from attending.

On May 3, 1916, after the death of Fritz Prastin of the *Eitel*, Thierichens requested permission to send a party ashore to conduct a funeral service. Rear Admiral Mclean allowed "10 officers, 14 warrant officers, 100 petty officers and men, and 13 men of the band…along with a firing squad consisting of 1 warrant officer, 1 petty officer and 30 men" to go to the Portsmouth Naval Hospital on May 4 to attend the funeral.[184] He gave the men approval to fire a volley over the grave during the service. McLean also gave them liberty to go to the hospital, but they had to march in one body and then return to the ship in formation.

Funeral observances during internment were a unique situation, because the United States allowed interned sailors to bear arms in order to fire a volley over the grave. Confined belligerents were given access to weapons and allowed to go outside of their restricted area. Such occurrences showed the extent to which the foreign sailors, U.S. military and local population were friendly and trustworthy toward one another.

The sailors regularly interacted with other interned German crews, both close by and farther afield. The SMS *Cormoran* was an example of the latter. On August 4, 1914, the German raider SMS *Emden* captured the Russian merchant ship *Cormoran* and quickly converted it into a merchant raider. The vessel left Tsingtao soon after conversion, and the *Cormoran* and the *Eitel* were sent to Australian waters to sink merchant ships. Admiral Maxmilian von Spee, German commander of the East Asia Squadron, believed that both ships were slow and burned too much coal to be effective. The *Cormoran* had a relatively uneventful journey before internment, but the *Eitel* destroyed eleven merchant ships before it eventually interned.[185] The *Cormoran* interned in Guam, a U.S. territory, after running low on fuel; the *Eitel* reached Hampton Roads.[186]

During the December 1915 holiday season, the crews of the *Eitel* and *Kronprinz* wished to send several items to the *Cormoran* interned in Guam. The list of Christmas presents included the following: "several magazines, 3 musical instruments, 5 packages of tobacco, 1 package of cigarettes, and 1 package of newspapers."[187] The items were cleared through customs and sent to Guam. Maintaining communication with other interned vessels was important for the crews of the *Eitel* and the *Kronprinz* to boost morale for their comrades during internment.

On February 1, 1916, the German steamship *Appam* sailed into Hampton Roads seeking refuge from British and French ships. The ship was a former British passenger liner that had been captured by the German cruiser SMS *Möwe*. Captain Nikolaus zu Dohna-Schlodien of the *Möwe* sent twenty-two of his men, including Lieutenant Hans Berg, to command the ship and control the *Appam*'s crew and passengers.

On its arrival, the U.S. government forced the *Appam* to release the British crew and passengers. The United States interned the German prize crew and placed them under Captain Thierichens's control.[188] Their ship was placed next to the *Eitel* and the *Kronprinz* in the navy yard, and Thierichens and the crew of the *Appam* became good friends.

On July 26, 1916, Thierichens requested the transfer of a cook and quartermaster from the *Eitel* to the *Appam*. According to the German captain, "When the *Appam* came in she had nobody onboard, who knew anything about cooking."[189] One of their sailors made the effort, but it was so bad

The SS *Appam* had a prize crew of twenty-two German sailors from the SMS *Möwe* when it entered Hampton Roads on February 1 seeking fuel and repairs. *Library of Congress.*

that it was not sufficient for the health of the crew.[190] Along with a cook, the *Appam* also needed a quartermaster to buy supplies. They were in need of someone "who knows the handling of buying foodstuff and who knows how to judge food stuffs," explained Thierichens.[191] McLean forwarded the request to Daniels. The secretary of the navy replied that they were not allowed to transfer a sailor from the *Eitel* to the *Appam*, but the *Appam*'s crew might visit the *Eitel* for any food needs.[192] It's unclear why Daniels denied the request, but despite the decision, Thierichens and Thierfelder would look out for the crew of the *Appam* throughout their internment. Their experience went hand in hand with that of the *Eitel* and the *Kronprinz*.

In July 1916, the German sailors were greatly surprised when the U-boat *Deutschland* arrived in Hampton Roads. Built by a private company and run by the North German Lloyd line, merchant submarines like the *Deutschland* were used as blockade runners. The *Deutschland* ran small shipments past Allied vessels in order to deliver essential goods to neutral and home ports. Captain Paul König and the crew of the *Deutschland* arrived in Hampton Roads on July 9, 1916, dropped off their cargo and planned to refuel and head back to Germany.[193] Their load, according to Captain König, was "a most valuable cargo of dyestuffs to our American friends, dyestuffs which have been so much needed for months in America and which the ruler of the seas has not allowed the great American Republic to import."[194] (German manufacturers dominated the synthetic textile dye industry, but the British blockade kept these products from entering U.S. markets.)

The "ruler of the seas" that König was referring to was England, and he proudly told American officials that Germany was developing more submarines that could easily sneak past Allied ships. The sub's cargo also included the interned sailors' mail. While the *Deutschland* was docked in Hampton Roads, the interned sailors threw its crew several parties. The sub's crew was honored on Sunday night in a celebration held onboard the *Eitel*. Lieutenant Berg of the *Appam* was an honored guest at this celebration.[195] The night before the U-boat left on August 3, 1916, the crews of the *Eitel* and the *Kronprinz* held another celebration to send off the successful crew and their commander. The guest of honor was Captain

One of two German merchant submarines, the *Deutschland* made two trips to the United States with a cargo of dyestuffs, mail and medical supplies. On the submarine's first journey to Baltimore, it also docked in Hampton Roads to deliver supplies and mail to the interned crews. Captain Thierichens hosted a party for the German submarine captain and crew. The *Deutschland* is shown at the Connecticut State Pier in New London for its second mission sometime between November 1 and 16, 1916. *Library of Congress.*

Hans Hinsch, commander of the German ship SS *Neckar*, which had been interned in Baltimore since the outbreak of the war. (The *Neckar* was a passenger and freight liner that sought refuge in the neutral U.S. port rather than be destroyed by Allied ships.) Hinsch toasted Captain König and the crew members of the sub, and the next day, the *Deutschland* left Hampton Roads and headed back to Bremen.[196]

The episode of the *Deutschland* was featured in the German sailors' newspaper. When the sub entered the Virginia Capes through the British blockade, the *Kolonie-Anzeiger* called the British captain "Blockade Captain of Cape Henry."[197] Then the paper poked fun at English culture, saying that "if you prefer your five o'clock tea we cannot help you." They did say that "the only information that we can give is that more such boats are to be expected."[198] The sailors sold issues of the *Kolonie-Anzeiger* to tourists, and the proceeds went to the German Red Cross.

The *Anzeiger*, which was published every Saturday, reported on daily war news that obviously favored the Germans and attempted to debunk British propaganda. The ten- to twelve-page newspaper also reported on events and happenings around the navy yard and provided some comic relief to the sailors' day-to-day routines. The publication discussed encouraging announcements, as when the ship received a delivery of ten kegs of beer from Herr Becker of Brooklyn, New York. One article reported that several ruffians who threw mud at the Germans during an opera performance were apprehended by local police.

The publication also listed want ads. For example, announcements for an errand boy, tailor's assistant and locksmith were featured in one edition. The printer also advertised a position that appeared to have narrow qualifications when he requested that the job be filled by two pretty young women with black hair.[199]

Fundraising opportunities and charity updates were also announced in the paper. The September 2, 1916 edition reported that, as of the previous issue, the collection for the blind was up to $223.58. Another interesting article showed the benevolent feelings that the local community had toward the crews of the *Eitel* and the *Kronprinz* when a sailor named Heinrich fell asleep in a trash can while doing laundry. The story recounted that the navy yard's trash collector, an African American man named Jimmy, found Heinrich and woke him up and helped him out before he was thrown into the incinerator. When Jimmy returned to work the next day, the German sailors gave him a standing ovation for saving their crew member.[200]

Published weekly by the German sailors, the *Kolonie-Anzeiger* provided comic relief, war news and happenings in the local community. This issue is from September 2, 1916. *Portsmouth Naval Shipyard Museum.*

Despite all of these social events, celebrations and sporting activities, the sailors were not free. Although they found activities to keep them busy during their internment, most of them longed to get back to their homeland.

# 5

# THE PROBLEMS OF INTERNMENT

## ESCAPES, PASSES AND THE SAGA OF THE *ECLIPSE*

Internment was not always a happy condition for the sailors. Many found the daily routine boring. They believed that, despite their positive interactions with locals and approved travel in Hampton Roads, they were still living in a foreign country against their will. No matter how comfortable their accommodations and how strong their ties to the local community, they still longed for freedom. Many sailors probably believed that the United States would eventually enter the war against Germany, and when that happened, they would become prisoners. Other sailors wanted to help the German war effort now. They had family and friends who were in the middle of the fighting, and they felt like they were doing nothing to assist. Others simply wanted to get a job, make money and start a new life under a different identity in the United States or abroad. All of these reasons are what led to the main problem of internment—escapes.

As soon as the ships arrived in Hampton Roads, there were reports of sailors leaving their interned area. On March 20, 1915, the *Virginian-Pilot* reported that several crew members of the *Eitel* left New York aboard the steamer *Hellig Olav*. The paper claimed that they arrived in Copenhagen with Swedish passports and that Thierichens gave them secret information to deliver to the German government.[201] One erroneous account said that the German captain was arrested in Paris disguised as a cook. Secretary of the Navy Daniels requested that Rear Admiral Beatty find Captain Thierichens's whereabouts immediately.[202] "Bosh," exclaimed Beatty. "None of the officers or crew have gone away since the vessel came here."[203]

Thierichens confirmed that all of the crew members were in Hampton Roads, and Collector of Customs Hamilton declared the rumors to be false. "The same number of men, [excepting] one who died as the result of an accident who were on board the vessel when she came here in March are still on board," reported Beatty.[204] He attested that since their arrival Thierichens reported the whereabouts of the crew members daily.[205] But confining the sailors to the navy yard would prove difficult for the German captains and the United States.

Less than a month after the *Eitel* interned, Lieutenant Otto Brauer disguised himself as a Russian sailor and boarded a Norwegian ship bound for Europe. He eventually made it back to Germany, where he became a torpedo officer aboard the SMS *Lutzow*.[206] The British found out that Brauer had escaped when they confiscated a letter from his mother to his brother Curt. Cecil Spring-Rice, British ambassador to the United States, later delivered it to Secretary of the Navy Daniels. The letter, dated August 19, 1915, explained that "Otto has had the most interesting experience of all" and was a member of the gunboat *Luchs* before he was ordered to board the *Eitel*.[207] The letter revealed her son's daring adventure aboard the raider, his internment in Hampton Roads and his escape back to Europe. Otto found life dull in the Virginia maritime community and wanted more action, so "he smuggled himself on board a Norwegian vessel as a 'Russian stoker', arrived safely and suddenly appeared in Berlin."[208] Frau Brauer was very proud of her son. "His courage was admired everywhere, and I was delighted to have my son with me again."[209]

Collector Hamilton granted parole to several officers on the ship before it was turned over to the United States. Daniels was upset to find out that Hamilton had granted permission without his approval and requested that paroles go through him in the future.[210] Thierichens claimed to have no idea that Brauer was missing. "Others have gone and they came back," explained the German captain.[211] Beatty argued that the missing sailor was not on the raider's roll when it interned. On "April 8th, 1915, Brauer not on list of officers at the time of internment, April 9, *Prinz Eitel* arrived at the Yard, April 13, Captain signed parole for himself, officers and crew."[212] Despite allegations that he left before the *Eitel* was interned, the fact was that the United States allowed a German sailor to escape, and this was unacceptable.

A few months after Brauer's disappearance, British officials detained a Dr. Nolte in Gibraltar in June 1915. Nolte was granted leave in May to visit Newport News and Old Point Comfort but failed to return. He left Hampton Roads under a Danish identity and boarded an Italian steamship,

There were fewer than fifty documented escape attempts during internment, around twenty of them successful. The escapes led to tighter restrictions and a constant battle between marine sentries and sailors. *Portsmouth Naval Shipyard Museum.*

SS *Tomaso Di Savoia.*[213] Thierichens was aware that Nolte was missing but had no idea he was in Gibraltar. Cecil Spring-Rice "indicat[ed] the advisability of further precaution in preventing the disappearance of the officers and men of the *Prinz Eitel Friedrich* and the *Kronprinz Wilhelm*, and I venture therefore to express the hope that, if the facts as stated are confirmed by any injuries which may be made by the US authorities, adequate measure will be taken in future to obviate the possibility of further escapes from the interned vessels."[214] Unfortunately for the British and the Americans, the escapes did not lessen—they increased.

On the morning of October 10, 1915, six interned sailors left the navy yard dressed in civilian clothes and embarked on a yacht, slipping past coastal guards off Cape Henry, and headed south. They had purchased the fifty-nine-foot vessel from Norfolk resident Benjamin F. Mitchell in September. The craft, which they named the *Eclipse*, was built in 1881 and could do a speed of around four knots.[215] The group worked on the boat for a month and equipped it with "new sails and several coats of paint, engine with twice the horsepower of the original."[216] They had become regulars at the local yacht club and had been out several times but had always returned.

Sir Cecil Spring-Rice served as British ambassador to the United States during World War I. *Library of Congress.*

Collector Hamilton wrote to Secretary of the Treasury William Gibbs McAdoo in September requesting permission for them to purchase the craft for recreational boating exercises and "that as soon as the transfer is made the vessel's document will be surrendered and bill of sale place[d] on record at this office."[217] McAdoo approved the purchase but was interested in getting the local officials' view on the subject. Beatty explained that he had "no valid objection to the ownership by the Germans of the yacht in question, as long as we are assured that the limitations are such that no additional information of military value is gained."[218] The commandant also listed several other stipulations. Sailing routes must be mapped out on the chart, and they could not be changed unless there was bad weather. Sailors must also receive permission if they wanted to go beyond Thimble Shoal Light. According to Beatty, this limit was designated so that they were "not being near our target practice ground in Tangier Sound, mouth of Potomac… while ships are firing."[219] Obviously, allowing the sailors to purchase a yacht was not in the United States' best interest.

Thierfelder was in denial when he found out that six of his men had left. "I do not believe they have escaped, but I cannot account for their absence."[220] In order to cooperate with local officials, he quickly provided a list of the men on the *Eclipse*.[221] The missing men were Lieutenant Heinrich Rudebüsch, Lieutenant Heinrich (Heinz) Hoffman, Lieutenant William Forstreuter, Lieutenant Erich (Emil) Biermann, Julius Lustfield and Walter Fischer. All of the men were between the ages of twenty-five and thirty.[222] Daniels believed that the yacht received gas rations from the *Kronprinz*.[223] Thierfelder staunchly rejected these accusations: "I stand for that it would be absolutely impossible to take off provisions out of the ship in such quantities as necessary for a longer trip at sea, without allowance."[224] He declared that the *Eitel* and the *Kronprinz* had only enough supplies to last a short period of time, so crews of the interned cruisers had to watch them carefully and would notice if any were missing.

The adventure of the *Eclipse* sparked several rumors concerning its whereabouts. An account from R.G. Thomas, an employee of the Branch Hydrographic Office, reported information from a local boatman, Howard S. Hudgins, who spotted the craft on October 10. According to Thomas, the wind was twenty-five miles per hour, the vessel had no additional weight and "she was poorly handled to the extent that she was in danger of being capsized."[225] His observation concluded that "the crew that sailed her from opposite Merritt & Chapman's to Craney Island were a dangerous crew to handle any boat, even a fine keeled boat, and that if they continued to sail her they probably capsized."[226]

There were also tales that the ship had been equipped with guns off the coast of Florida and joined up with a raiding party to sink British and French vessels. Other testimonies claimed that the crew of the *Eclipse* had joined a Swedish steamer off Texas and went to Cuba or Mexico. Two bottles washed upon the Virginia beaches with messages from the *Eclipse*. The first message read, "On Board Yacht *Eclipse*, ninety miles off Hatteras in howling gale, no water and no gasoline, everyone exhausted."[227] The next message was found off Ocean View by Clark Weaton. Weaton, of Chicago, Illinois, was walking on the beach and came across a champagne bottle that contained the message, "We are sailing for Germany on the yacht *Eclipse* from 6 of the German ship lying in the U.S. Navy Yard."[228] Beatty believed the tales were probably false; it was most likely that they were either picked up by a British ship or drowned at sea. Thierfelder agreed and said that his sailors weren't stupid and that he believed the letters were fakes.

Reports continued that the *Eclipse* was spotted off the Virginia coast. On October 15, 1915, Captain Benjamin M. Chiswell alleged to have seen a "yacht answering to description of *Eclipse* fishing off Taft Rappahannock River today moved up river four PM now off Taft will search up river at daylight."[229] Three days later, another account from Virginia Beach Naval Radio Compass Station sighted a white boat fitting the description of the *Eclipse* four miles offshore moving southeast.[230] Norfolk resident W.P. Allen responded that there is "not truth in the rumor" that the vessel was the *Eclipse*, because the white yacht was his family's boat.[231] Several captains of private ships off the coast stated that they had seen no boat resembling the *Eclipse* but admitted that the vessel could have easily slipped by in the fog. The naval stations still believed that the vessel made it through the Virginia Capes and was on its way to the Florida coast.[232] The *New York Times* even reported that the Germans had left the Virginia coast and were bound for Cuba.[233] Unfortunately for the German sailors, neither the missing boat nor its crew was ever found.

The saga of the *Eclipse* was an embarrassment for Beatty and the U.S. government. The commandant sent orders to Thierichens that "no further leave or furlough will be granted until further orders."[234] Franklin Roosevelt, assistant secretary of the navy, reiterated the importance of the situation by asking Beatty to "Recall officers and men of interned German ships now on leave….Grant leave no further."[235] Guests and visitors were denied access to the sailors and were only permitted with signed passes from the commanding officers between 8:00 a.m. and sunset.[236] The process for how the sailors requested leave was changed immediately. Originally, they needed permission from only their own captain, but after the incident with the *Eclipse*, the U.S. government required more control over these permits.[237] In the future, sailors had to get permission from not only their captain but also the commandant of the Norfolk Navy Yard.

The sailors' hours for activities were also limited to 8:00 a.m. to sunset. Beatty only allowed the men to go ashore to their village if they were

Sailing was a major part of the interned sailors' activities. The six of the *Eclipse* became regulars at the local yachting club and had been out several times before but had always come back. The saga of the *Eclipse* would change the way paroles worked for the sailors. They could only go ashore in small groups, and their sailing time was limited. *Portsmouth Naval Shipyard Museum.*

escorted by reliable officers and returned immediately to the ship.[238] He wanted to prevent unauthorized departures and maintain strict control and accountability of the sailors.

The restrictions did not stop escapes, because shortly after the *Eclipse* slipped out of Hampton Roads, two other sailors, Dr. Kruger Kroneck and Lieutenant Koch, fled the navy yard. The officers had received leave to visit New York City and Niagara Falls from September 29, 1915, to October 16, 1915, but failed to return. Search parties were dispatched, but the police did not find any sign of them in the surrounding areas. A Red Cross transport commander reported that he saw them on October 17 at Pennsylvania Station in New York, when they said goodbye and announced that they would return to the German raider.[239] "They have violated their parole," wrote Beatty to Secretary of the Navy Daniels, "under which circumstance which, as presented believed to be true, are especially embarrassing." Beatty, greatly angered over the disappearance of the two officers, believed that if escapes continued, the interned sailors would have to be treated as prisoners.[240]

On November 11, 1915, a sailor from the *Eitel* lowered himself down the side of the ship and swam to the swampy area of the navy yard. Thiery, a

Franklin Delano Roosevelt (*left*) was the assistant secretary of the navy from 1913 to 1920. *Library of Congress.*

twenty-five-year-old with a small frame, brown hair and brown eyes, left the ship sometime between 9:00 p.m. on Thursday and 6:00 a.m. on Friday. The crew assumed that he was sleeping and didn't notice he was missing until the next day. He had leave from July 25 to August 7 and returned, but Thierichens believed it was possible that, this time, he went back to his

Beatty created tighter restrictions around the navy yard after the escapes. Sailors were allowed to leave their ships only if escorted by reliable officers. They could only go to certain parts of the navy yard and to their houses and had to return to their ship. *Norfolk Public Library, Norfolk, Virginia.*

relatives in Michigan. The German captain included a picture of Thiery with two of his cousins and a woman and enclosed a drawing of the sailor's tattoo, which appeared on his lower right arm.[241] Once authorities were notified of the sailor's disappearance, boats and search parties went up and down the navy yard but could find no trace of the crew member.[242]

Authorities even expanded their search to Detroit in an attempt to find Thiery and his supposed acquaintance, a Mr. Spork. Beatty wired a description of Thiery to the Detroit chief of police. The sailor was listed as "stoker...brown eyes, teeth good, goatee and mustache, 70 inches, 135 pounds, age 25, poor English...tattooed."[243] The commandant believed Thiery was staying at 265 Lamothe Street in Detroit, but the chief of police checked the address and could not find either man.[244]

Beatty received a letter from a sheriff in Falls City, Nebraska, on November 18, 1915, claiming that he had a man who resembled Thiery. The sheriff noted that "there is a German that is working near here, and made the remark that he was a German soldier, or officer off of an interned ship."[245] Beatty responded that Thiery should be near or around the Detroit area. Nebraska was out of his probable area. The commandant sent a list with

The USS *Richmond* held one of the escaped sailors, Otto Buelow. The ship was built in 1860 and saw active service in the Civil War and was an auxiliary receiving ship at the Norfolk Navy Yard from 1903 until the end of World War I. *Library of Congress.*

detailed descriptions of nine of the missing crew members—Lieutenant Koch, Dr. Kruger Kroneck, Thiery, Heinrich Rudebüsch, Heinrich Hoffman, Wilhelm Forstreuter, Julius Lustfield and Walter Fischer—but none of the descriptions matched.[246] As they continued to look for Thiery, Beatty discovered that another sailor had disappeared.

On November 22, 1915, Beatty received word that Otto Buelow was missing. The commandant suspended all leave for the men. Thierichens told Beatty that he was embarrassed for his officers and crew that Buelow had escaped. On December 2, Secretary of the Navy Daniels told the commandant that the missing sailor was being held aboard the ship USS *Richmond*.[247] The steamer was built in 1860, had served in the Civil War and was now stationed in Hampton Roads as an auxiliary to the receiving vessel USS *Franklin*. The sailor, upset at being caught and now held aboard the U.S. vessel, wrote to Daniels requesting "to be informed why I am being held at this station and when I'll be released."[248] Buelow was eventually returned to the interned German cruiser.

There were fewer than fifty documented escape attempts, a small percentage compared to the total number of German sailors interned (eight hundred). The press didn't help the situation when it made false accusations that members of the *Eitel* and the *Kronprinz* were missing throughout the United States. Daniels wrote to Beatty in November to find out if a German man who had recently died in Pennsylvania was a member of one of the crews. The secretary of the navy forwarded the newspaper clipping that stated that Frank Albert Wurstier, a member of the *Eitel*, had been killed by a Lehigh Valley Railroad freight train near White Haven, Pennsylvania.[249] Thierichens said the article was false and "a man called Frank Albert Wurstier has never been on board the Eitel or Wilhelm."[250] In another false accusation, Baltimore police arrested a German whom they suspected was a crew member of the *Eitel*. The authorities attested that he was Petty Officer Unger from one of the German raiders. They brought him to the navy yard, where Beatty denied that Unger was a member of the German cruiser.[251] There were even false accusations in the local paper. In November, the *Virginian-Pilot and the Norfolk Landmark* commented that "since they arrived it is believed that more than 100 members of the interned ships have escaped."[252] This exaggeration (there were fewer than fifty documented escapes) showed the obsession of the local populations with the escapes. As a result of the missing sailors, along with the false accusations, Daniels relayed orders to Beatty that the "department desires any steps to prevent further escapes should be taken in such a manner as to avoid publicity or comment."[253]

Of the roughly fifty documented escapes, fewer than half of the sailors concerned were not returned to the navy yard. No matter how well the German sailors were treated by the local population and U.S. Navy officials, a small number of them were not deterred from attempting to escape. Major motives for escapes included not only the boredom of internment, but also the idea that the sailors' family, friends and country were suffering across the ocean. Brauer was one example of a sailor who escaped and then quickly rejoined the German navy so he could fight for his country again. Lieutenant Wilhelm Forstreuter, one of the members of the *Eclipse*, had learned that his family's home was overrun by the Russians and hadn't heard from them since he arrived in Hampton Roads. His decision to join the *Eclipse* was a direct result of his family's circumstances. Some sailors escaped not to get back to Germany but to stay in the United States as free men. If they had relatives in America, they escaped to visit with them. A few sailors obtained overnight passes to visit relatives in other states and never returned. No matter the sailors' reasons for escaping, the United States needed to do something to stop them.

# 6

# A Change in the Guard

With continued false reports from the media on escape attempts and the lingering effects of the episode of the *Eclipse*, Washington became more involved in the situation in Hampton Roads. Roosevelt demanded that all crew members have their pictures taken and filed for security purposes: "it is essential that the secret service obtain proofs of the identity of the officers and crews now on board."[254] Secretary of State Lansing requested that sailors go ashore for only essential purposes, such as mail deliveries, livestock feeding, performing drill or if proper passes had been acquired from their captain and commandant.[255] Daniels told Beatty that even with these exceptions it was essential to maintain strict guard over the sailors to avoid any future escapes.[256] He reiterated that the "department desires most seriously to impress upon you [Beatty] that recurrence of such escapes would create situations of great gravity and could not be excused."[257] Washington was upset with the escapes and expected a change. The United States was attempting to maintain a policy of strict neutrality; allowing belligerents to escape from U.S. custody did not look good in terms of security or public appearance and showed that the United States lacked control and revealed to the Allies that the nation was not able to keep its enemy confined.

On November 26, 1915, the *Virginian-Pilot and the Norfolk Landmark* reported that Beatty would retire by the end of the month. He arranged to "go to Charleston for a few days and then plans on retiring in D.C. where he will work on creating a more formidable navy to protect the coast."[258]

Rear Admiral Walter McLean took over as commander of the Norfolk Navy Yard on November 25, 1915. McLean would become close friends with Niezychowski and encourage him to write a book on the *Kronprinz*'s journey at sea. McLean wrote the foreword to his book and was the best man in Niezychowski's wedding. *Library of Congress.*

Rear Admiral Walter McLean took over Beatty's position as commandant of the Norfolk Navy Yard at the end of November 1915. McLean was a graduate of the U.S. Naval Academy who had served on Admiral George Dewey's staff in the Asiatic theater and also on Washington's naval advisory board. He had been promoted to rear admiral in 1914 and then given command of a portion of the Atlantic Fleet.[259] McLean's goal for his new assignment was to control the escapes, but he also wanted to establish trust between the sailors and U.S. officials.

The November 29, 1915 edition of the *Washington Post* reported that Thierichens "engaged in a wordy dispute with one of the Yard sentries on post near his vessel as a result of which the sentry's face was slapped by Capt. Thierichens."[260] McLean defended the German captain, stating that the story was false and that "Thierichens, or not one of his officers or men, has been connected with no incident in connection with Yard authorities that gives the slightest warrant for the story published in the [P]ost."[261] McLean's defense of the captain showed that he was willing to protect the German visitors.

The escapes lessened during McLean's watch but did not completely stop. On November 28, 1915, Ernest Schnetzker slid down the side of the *Kronprinz* unobserved, swam against a strong tide to Berkley, reached shore and then boarded the ferry to Norfolk. Schnetzker was spotted by a local mill worker, who quickly informed the authorities. The next night, they followed his tracks, which led them down Water Street, where they found him soaking wet, huddled next to a stove.[262] One of Schnetzker's friends admitted that he had heard him talking about leaving the week before when he had been drinking heavily.[263] To try to curtail this type of escape, the senior officer present afloat, E.A. Anderson (Anderson served as supervisor of Naval Auxiliary Reserves, Norfolk), ordered the commanding officers of the ships closest to the *Eitel* and the *Wilhelm* (USS *Delaware* and USS *Vermont*) "to increase vigilant lookout to prevent further escapes."[264]

In January 1916, four sailors escaped in the same manner as had Schnetzker, but they were able to make it to Wilmington, Delaware, where they found employment. Some of the sailors were interested in making more money for themselves and/or for their family, so they located other areas of employment after they escaped. For many sailors, the potential for finding work or passage back to Germany and family and friends outweighed the consequences of being captured. Karl Altman and Emil Klappstein started working on a U.S. ship, the *Minquas*, and the other two sailors, Fred Kruger and Karl Graham, joined the local textile plant. Their time in Delaware was brief; some local residents reported them to the authorities. All four were eventually arrested and sent back to the *Kronprinz*.[265]

It was the marine sentries' duty to check permits, and the guards didn't always get along with the interned sailors. Soon after they arrived, Thierfelder explained that the guards posed a threat to the original agreement between the Americans and the German ship, because they did not allow guests aboard the *Kronprinz* even when they had the proper papers.[266] The German captain complained that "the sentry on drydock II does not let pass these visitors, even if the officer goes personally to the sentry and accompanies his guests on board."[267] Thierfelder hoped that visitors would be allowed to gain access if they were accompanied by officers, but the U.S. Navy reiterated that there were strict orders regarding access to the raiders. Only visitors with the proper documentation by the captain and commandant would be allowed on the ship.[268]

The sentries were also in charge of enforcing the rules of leave. On November 24, 1915, fifteen sailors went ashore to feed livestock in the

The U.S. Marines controlled the checkpoints and sometimes posed a problem for the German sailors when they wanted to invite guests. The sentries were not very consistent; sometimes they would let guests through with proper documentation. At other times, they didn't. *Library of Congress.*

village. They were halted by marines, and Private Timothy J. Kelly told the sailors that they needed to have an escort and could only go to shore in groups of five or fewer. The men took off toward the livestock when Kelly approached them, but two marines were able to stop the sailors. The marines were worried that the sailors would retaliate, especially after one sailor attempted to get free again and there was almost a scuffle. The marines successfully apprehended the men but tried to avoid physical altercations as much as possible.[269]

The confrontations between sentries and sailors continued into December. On December 8, 1915, some of the crew members encountered a drunk marine guarding their ship. The corporal in charge discovered the intoxicated marine and quickly moved him off guard duty and into his quarters.[270] Thierichens wrote to McLean and explained that this behavior was unacceptable and that there should be consequences for the guard's irresponsible actions.[271] The rear admiral then contacted H.C. Snyder, commanding officer of the marines, and recommended that the drunken marine, Timothy J. Kelly, be discharged.[272]

McLean continued to exhibit goodwill toward the German sailors. He attempted to give the sailors comfortable and relaxing living conditions to gain their trust. Trust was a major part of what McLean was trying to establish with the crews of the *Eitel* and the *Kronprinz*, and if there were disorderly sentries, that trust could be affected. He also continued to form strong bonds with the men, especially Niezychowski and some of the other officers.

On July 24, 1916, the sailors got their revenge on the sentries when Warrant Officer Bettcher was shooting sparrows in the navy yard with a Flobert air rifle and accidently hit one of the guards on duty. McLean responded immediately with instructions to Thierfelder to eliminate the use of such weapons within the internment camp.[273] Even though the marines' checkpoints created problems when they verified documentation, the ultimate decision for passes was up to the commandant of the navy yard, and family passes were always a sensitive matter.

Once interned, some of the sailors made arrangements for their families to move from Germany to Hampton Roads, but it was difficult for the sailors to see them because of pass restrictions. In November 1915, Lieutenant Mueller requested authorization for his wife and children. They had permits for the main gate but wanted easier access, so he asked for them to be able to pass through a gate that was closer.[274] According to the German officer, "As I am now kept to the ship my wife will change her home to Portsmouth

Several of the sailors arranged for their families to move from Germany to the United States. *Library of Congress.*

because the children are small and it is very hard for her to come over to the ship with children to see me."[275]

Another sailor wished to meet his wife, who had recently landed in New York on a Dutch vessel. She spoke no English, and the sailor hoped he would be able to visit her when she arrived in Hampton Roads. Rear Admiral Beatty relayed the message to Daniels and responded that he "cannot permit deviation from decision already given concerning leave for interned officers."[276] The strict rules regarding passes was an ongoing frustration for the sailors.

Engineer Albert Warnecke's wife moved to the Norfolk area soon after the merchant raider's arrival. On November 4, 1915, Secretary of the Navy Daniels denied Warnecke's appeal for shore leave to see her. In January 1916, the sailor asked once again for leave to visit his wife. Thierichens requested permission for Warnecke to travel to Norfolk to assist his wife with purchasing another home.[277] The same day as Warnecke's appeal, the German captain also appealed for Mueller's authorization to see his sick wife in Norfolk. The tightening of the passes began to show the changing feeling of the United States for German aliens and interned sailors.

Thierichens continued to write requests for sailors to see other family members in the area or for their families to come on the ship. On February 18, 1916, he asked for clearance for paymaster Lessau to meet his two cousins in the area. McLean responded that he could not allow the sailor to accompany his cousins to their hotel, but he was allowed to take them to the navy yard entrance, where they could get in their car.[278]

Dr. Schler was one of the crew members who had a flexible permit. Because he was a medical doctor, he was allowed to go to lectures and visit other ships, hospitals and doctors throughout Hampton Roads. He could travel "through and out of navy yard anytime, for purpose of going to Norfolk or Portsmouth to communicate with doctors, apothecaries, and hospitals on duty connected with the interned German vessels at the Yard."[279] Commander Thierichens reinforced the importance of Schler's freedom, stressing that he should be able to go to the designated locations any day or night, because "he's the only surgeon on board both ships and he must be able to personally communicate with any surgeon, apothecary and hospitals, and to be at present at any scientific lectures in medical societies seeming to him of his interest."[280]

McLean, like Beatty, used rewards to try to increase the probability of apprehending sailors. On May 25, 1916, he posted a description of a missing crew member: "Friedrich Heinrich Wilhelm Schulz…steward, medium sized, blonde hair, and a scar on his right gold [ring] finger."[281] Schulz had left the interned area when he was supposedly visiting the dentist. There was a compensation of fifty dollars if he was returned within sixty days. According to McLean, "The reward shall be in full satisfaction of all expensed for arresting, keeping, and delivering such deserter or straggler."[282] Thierichens believed the sailor had gone to find work aboard another steamer, because he had complained about his pay aboard the *Eitel*. Several months later, McLean reported to Daniels that Schulz had been captured in Baltimore on September 8; he was delivered to *Eitel* the next day.[283]

Despite Schulz's and the other escapes, McLean showed sympathy for the men by requesting that they be given more liberty during the summer to use beach resorts and engage in field activities. The commandant believed that these options would be helpful, since the sailors were not used to the humid summer heat of Virginia. The resorts included Ocean View and even private beaches. Owners at Willoughby Spit, "a largely private beach and not so accessible as is Ocean view…indicated their willingness to permit the use

A 1915 blueprint of the Norfolk Navy Yard. The sailors' village occupied the unused area south and southwest of Dry Dock 3. *Portsmouth Naval Shipyard Museum.*

of their premises by parties from the interned ships."[284] The cooperation of the members of a private beach community to allow access to foreign sailors showed how comfortable the local community was with having interned sailors there. They gave the crews of the *Eitel* and the *Kronprinz* access to their beach, while some members of the general public could not enter. The community saw the German sailors as welcome guests and wanted to help accommodate them.

If approved, small parties of sailors could be transported to the beach, where an officer would keep watch over them. In his letter to Secretary of the Navy Daniels, McLean explained that "granting this extended liberty is most desirable and quite necessary to their health and contentment of the interned." He also said that he did not think that the interned men would break parole if given more liberty to go to shore resorts.[285] Daniels did not agree with McLean's optimistic outlook and denied the request for increased leave. He said that he would gladly allow them, but there was no guarantee that they would not leave. The secretary of the navy was right, because there was an escape attempt the very next day.

On August 8, 1916, three sailors attempted to leave the navy yard by swimming across the river. The men started from the athletic field and were quickly spotted by a sentry, who escorted them back to the raider.[286] McLean, upset that they got away, requested that "in the future when the athletic field is in use by your men, please see that reliable petty officers [are] present to

*Above and opposite page*: On September 29, 1916, the ships were moved to Philadelphia to make room for the expansion of the Norfolk Navy Yard. The sailors' village was torn down, and the sailors were relocated to Philadelphia. *Norfolk Public Library, Norfolk, Virginia. Historic Norfolk Navy Yard glass plate negative collection.*

prevent any further occurrences."[287] Less than a month later, they would have another chance to stop an escape.

In September 1916, German officers redeemed themselves by successfully stopping a fellow sailor from leaving. McLean praised the actions of the guards. "The watchfulness and activity of the Germans in this case was most commendable, but was in line with what I had reason to expect and was altogether in accord with my personal understanding with the German commanding officer, that in somewhat extending the limits and freedom of the internment camp, he should have selected men of his command on duty within the camp to preserve order and assist our own meager guard in preventing any straggling beyond the prescribed limits."[288]

McLean was happy that the German sailors successfully prevented their own man from escaping. He had gained their trust and even formed

*This page and opposite*: Many Norfolk and Portsmouth residents were sad to see the German sailors move to Philadelphia. Their presence on the streets, in shops, at baseball games and at church services would be missed. Their village was an icon in the Hampton Roads area and served as a major part of Norfolk and Portsmouth tourism. *Virginia Historical Society (2002.367.12), Hampton Roads Naval Museum.*

strong friendships with some of the men. He became good friends with Count Alfred von Niezychowski, and they would continue correspondence throughout their lives. Unfortunately for the sailors and McLean, the *Eitel* and the *Wilhelm* would be moved temporarily to Philadelphia to make room for the expansion of the Norfolk Navy Yard, and many of the friendships would come to an end.

Naval officials determined in the summer of 1916 that the Norfolk Navy Yard would be expanded. The sailors had to tear down the village that had taken them almost six months to create. Representatives of the navy yard reported that it would take at least $25,000 to re-create the beloved attraction. The community made it clear that it would be missed. "The German village at the Norfolk, Virginia, navy yard is no more, and the whole South is the sufferer thereby," exclaimed one article in *Popular Science*.[289]

The people of Hampton Roads embraced the foreign sailors and enjoyed their company, so much so that the Germans became permanent fixtures in their community. The almost daily reports that came from the local paper showed that nearby residents loved their German guests. The interned sailors purchased goods and attended social events throughout the city. The sailors were invited to their homes, churches and sporting events. But once the ships were moved out of Hampton Roads and the United States was closer to entering World War I, the positive relationship between the German sailors and U.S. citizens seemed unlikely to be sustained.

# EPILOGUE

O
n September 29, 1916, U.S. authorities moved the German sailors to the Philadelphia Navy Yard (League Island). A decision that had been debated since the sailors' arrival had now come to pass. The transfer of the interned cruisers to Philadelphia was a delicate process. Washington had to make sure that the Germans would not escape, and U.S. officials needed to provide protection from British and French ships. Rear Admiral McLean made sure that the cruisers were loaded with only enough coal to make it to their new home, so that they would not have an opportunity to flee. Washington also ensured that the former merchant raiders were safeguarded from Allied ships by providing an escort to the mouth of the Delaware Bay that included cruisers and destroyers. The German vessels made their way up the Delaware River and into League Island—their new place of internment.[290]

The German sailors' time in Philadelphia was shorter and not as lenient as their stay in Hampton Roads, as strains on German-American relations had increased. By the beginning of 1917, skepticism about German immigrants and interned sailors began to spread after incidents in the Northeast, where German aliens sabotaged U.S. property. Rumblings in the Philadelphia community of a potential backlash against the interned sailors forced Secretary Daniels to transfer the Germans to a more secure barracks for their own protection from the possibility of Philadelphia mobs. Mayor Thomas B. Smith of Philadelphia expressed his trepidations about keeping the crew members of the *Eitel* and the *Kronprinz* in his city. "They might

*This page*: The German ships *Eitel* and *Kronprinz* were transferred to Philadelphia on September 29, 1916, to make room for the Norfolk Navy Yard expansion. *Hampton Roads Naval Museum*.

all escape and seize the navy yard....At the very least, they were all spying against America."[291] Mayor Smith had a rational concern, because on March 20, Victor Korth and thirteen other sailors, assuming that they would be imprisoned within the next few weeks, escaped from League Island. Of these, four were captured and returned to the internment area.[292] To alleviate the concerns about protecting the German sailors' safety and U.S. property,

The interned sailors' new home was Philadelphia, where their experience would not be as congenial as it had been in Hampton Roads. Diplomatic relations between Germany and America became more strained. *Courtesy of Paul H. Silverstone, 1983. U.S. Naval History and Heritage Command Photograph.*

Washington decided to move the sailors south to a more secluded prison barracks, away from ocean access, at Fort Oglethorpe and Fort McPherson in Georgia. (A small number of sailors stayed with the ships until the United States entered the war.) Their new homes featured greater isolation from civilian populations and from water access and stronger security, provided by the Seventeenth Infantry. Both of these factors made escapes and sabotage extremely difficult.

On April 6, 1917, after a series of disputes with Germany over unrestricted submarine warfare, the United States entered World War I against the German Empire. That same day, the collector of internal revenue for the Port of Philadelphia seized the interned cruisers. The crew members of the surface raiders officially became prisoners of war. Now enemies of the United States and not friends of the local community, the sailors did not have the same opportunities as they had when they were interned in Hampton Roads.[293] Their freedom of movement and liberties were stripped.

U.S. officials quickly created massive anti-German propaganda to bolster the war effort. Advertisements and slogans labeled the Germans as "Huns" and "Barbarians" willing to kill women and children. The anti-German hysteria was far from the feelings that the Hampton Roads residents and navy yard officials had experienced in the spring of 1915, when the *Eitel* and the *Kronprinz* arrived. According to Rear Admiral McLean, the German sailors "had the same sense of chivalry on which we prided ourselves, and which distinguishes civilized warfare from the fighting of barbarism."[294] Despite the unique experience for the residents of Hampton Roads, the hostility toward all things German took hold. German street names were changed and businesses were boycotted, including German beer companies. German food became unpopular, and German books were outlawed. The hospitality and kindness the German sailors had experienced in Hampton Roads before 1917 became a distant memory when America entered the war in April. The sailors were not the "Kaiser's courteous pirates" but were now considered barbarians.

On May 22, 1917, President Woodrow Wilson delivered Executive Order 2624 concerning the German raiders, and the secretary of the navy took possession of the interned cruisers.[295] The *Kronprinz Wilhelm* was renamed the USS *Von Steuben* and continued service as an armed merchant ship for the United States. Due to growing demand for troop transports, the ship was reconditioned to meet the need to ferry American armed forces to Europe. The vessel had an adventurous career as a troop transport and was scrapped in 1923. The *Eitel* was also outfitted and reconditioned as a troop transport ship and renamed USS *Dekalb*. Ironically, the *Eitel* and the *Wilhelm* were renamed after Revolutionary War officers who had ties to Germany. After successful service as a troop transport during the war, the *Eitel* returned to public service as SS *Mount Clay* and served as a transatlantic liner until 1925. The ship was scrapped in 1934.[296]

The sailors' two years of confinement to Fort Oglethorpe and Fort McPherson was dull compared to their experience in Hampton Roads. The crew members of the *Eitel* and the *Wilhelm* were among more than 1,000 German naval officers and sailors transferred from various internment locations. Other enemy-alien camps included Fort Hot Springs in North Carolina and Fort Douglas in Utah. These camps also housed German merchantmen from luxury liners and cargo ships who were interned in U.S. ports, along with alien enemy subjects.[297] The German POWs were released in 1919, a few months after the end of the war. Most went back home to Europe, but some sailors enjoyed their stay so much that they decided to make the United States their permanent home. Of 173 German naval prisoners who applied for permission to remain in the country, 77 were allowed to stay.[298]

Sheet music entitled "Old Satan Gets the Hun." This anti-German propaganda shows the devil pushing Kaiser Wilhelm II into the fire. *Library of Congress*.

Count Alfred von Niezychowski was one of the men permitted to stay in the United States. The former German naval officer from the *Kronprinz* became a U.S. citizen in January 1926, and he married socialite Nanine H. Ulman of Baltimore on December 27, 1927.[299] Niezychowski's choice for his

*This page*: When the United States entered the war, it converted the raiders into troop transports. The *Eitel* was renamed USS *Dekalb* (*top*), and the *Kronprinz* was renamed the USS *Von Steuben* (*bottom*). *U.S. Naval History and Heritage Command.*

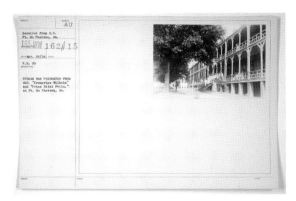

*Left*: Once America entered the war, the sailors became prisoners of war at Fort Oglethorpe and Fort McPherson in Georgia. This is an image of their barracks at Fort McPherson, where they would live for the next two years.

*Below*: POWs at Fort McPherson make souvenirs to sell, April 1918. *U.S. National Archives and Records Administration.*

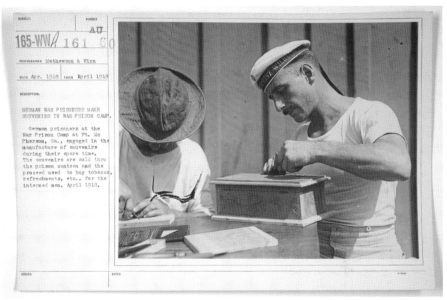

best man at his wedding may have surprised many because of the past strain on German-American relations since American entry into World War I. But to those who knew about the internment, it may not have been such a shock. His best man was retired U.S. Navy officer Rear Admiral Walter McLean, who had watched Niezychowski and the rest of the eight hundred German sailors from the two interned ships.

Two years after his wedding in 1929, Niezychowski published a book about his experience aboard the *Kronprinz Wilhelm*. In the foreword of *The Cruise of the Kronprinz Wilhelm*, Walter McLean, his best man and the overseer of the German sailors, explained that "the *Wilhelm* was a

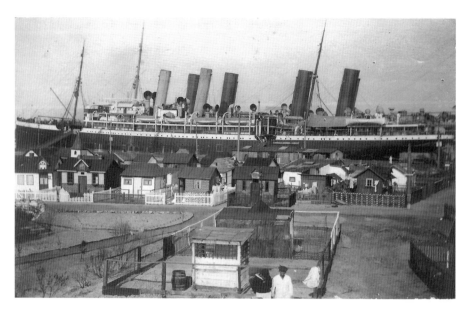

Hampton Roads was a "Haven of Safety" for the crews of the *Eitel* and the *Kronprinz* during World War I. *Portsmouth Naval Shipyard Museum.*

friendly visitor [and] Count von Niezychowski…became my guest."[300] Positive relationships like that between Niezychowski and McLean echoed throughout their stay at Hampton Roads. These bonds are what made the internment of the *Prinz Eitel Friedrich* and the *Kronprinz Wilhem* so unique.

The story of the German sailors interned in Hampton Roads demonstrates that, given the right circumstances, people were able to get beyond stereotypes and fears and connect culturally. It can be easy to understand and embrace the exciting and daring adventures of a ship's journey, but what happens to the sailors after the battles are over? The German sailors' internment was just as important as their voyage at sea. The internment of the *Prinz Eitel Friedrich* and the *Kronprinz Wilhelm* sheds light on a missing chapter in the study of war and society. Niezychowski's conclusion to his book echoes these thoughts, and it is what made me realize that there was a great story behind that postcard I had found in the stacks of the Virginia Historical Society. He said, "the events of our internment were as interesting to me as those of the cruise."[301] I believe Niezychowski was right.

# NOTES

## Chapter 1

1. *Virginian-Pilot and the Norfolk Landmark*, March, 29, 1915.
2. Ibid.
3. Ibid.
4. Ibid.
5. James Brown Scott, "The Escape of Paroled Members of the Crews of the Interned Cruisers in the United States," *American Journal of International Law* 10, no. 4 (1916): 878.
6. Ibid.
7. Lieutenant Commander Brumby and Rear Admiral Fiske, telephone conversation, March, 10, 1915, "*Prinz Eitel Friedrich and Kronprinz Wilhelm,*" Entry 520 in Inventory 18, *Inventory of the Naval Records Collection of the Office of Naval Records and Library*, RG 45-JT Enemy Naval Ships other than U-boats, National Archives and Records Administration, Washington, D.C. (hereafter NARA).
8. *Virginian-Pilot and the Norfolk Landmark*, April 4, 1915.
9. The Postcard and Ephemera Collection of Jeff Newman, Narrative by Mark Baber, http://www.greatships.net/kwilhelmdergrosse.html.
10. Robert K. Massie, *Castles of Steel: Britain, Germany, and the Winning of the Great War at Sea* (New York: Random House, 2003), 285.
11. John Bach McMaster, *United States in the World War* (New York: D. Appleton and Company, 1918), 83–84.

12. *Virginian-Pilot and the Norfolk Landmark*, March 11, 1915.

13. Massie, 241.

14. *Virginian-Pilot and the Norfolk Landmark*, March 11, 1915.

15. Massie, 235.

16. David M. Kennedy, *Over Here: The First World War and American Society* (New York: Oxford, 1980), 381.

17. *Virginian-Pilot and the Norfolk Landmark*, March 19, 1915.

18. Ibid., March 1, 1915.

19. Norman R. Hamilton, director of the Norfolk Banks of Savings and Trusts and former newspaper editor, became collector of customs on April 16, 1914. *Encyclopedia of Virginia* (New York: Lewis Historical Publishing Company, 1915), 4:377.

20. *Virginian-Pilot and the Norfolk Landmark*, April 12, 1915.

21. Ibid.

22. Daniels to Government Flag Officer, *Alabama*, March 27, 1915, NARA.

23. *Virginian-Pilot and the Norfolk Landmark*, March 27, 1915.

24. Daniels to Government Flag Officer, *Alabama*, March 31, 1915, NARA.

25. Captain of Coast Artillery Corps to Commanding Officer at Fort Monroe, March 27, 1915, NARA.

26. *Virginian-Pilot and the Norfolk Landmark*, March 28, 1915. The Hague Conventions of 1899 and 1907 were two conferences held at the Hague in the Netherlands where international leaders set up laws and guidelines concerning war and war crimes.

27. Daniels to Norfolk Navy Yard, March 25, 1915, NARA.

28. *Virginian-Pilot and the Norfolk Landmark*, March 28, 1915. Schedule: Saturday, March 27, British 3, French 1; Friday, March 26, British 6; Thursday March 25, British 7; Wednesday, March 24, British 2; March 23, British 1; Monday, March 22, British 2; March 21, British 2.

29. *Virginian-Pilot and the Norfolk Landmark*, April 6, 1915.

30. Ibid., April 1, 1915.

31. Ibid.

32. Ibid.

33. Ibid.

34. Ibid., March 27, 1915.

35. Ibid.

36. Ibid., April 1, 1915.

37. Ibid.

38. Ibid., April 5, 1915.

39. Ibid.

40. Hamilton to Thierichens, March 20, 1915, NARA.

41. Ibid.

42. Ibid., April 7, 1915, NARA.

43. Thierichens to Hamilton, April 8, 1915, NARA.

44. Ibid.

45. Ibid.

46. *Virginian-Pilot and the Norfolk Landmark*, April 8, 1915.

47. Ibid.

48. Ibid.

49. Ibid.

50. Ibid.

51. Ibid.

52. Ibid.

53. Ibid., April 9, 1915.

54. Edwin P. Hoyt, *Ghost of the Atlantic: the Kronprinz Wilhelm, 1914–1919* (London: Arthur Barker Limited, 1974), 106.

55. Count Alfred von Niezychowski, *The Cruise of the Kronprinz Wilhelm* (New York: Sun Dial Press, 1938), 292.

56. Ibid., 293.

57. Niezychowski, *Cruise of the Kronprinz Wilhelm*, 294.

58. Ibid., 295.

59. Ibid.

60. Ibid., 296.

61. Ibid., 297–98.

62. Ibid., 298.

63. Ibid., 299.

64. University of Maryland Medical Center, "Beriberi Overview," http://www.umm.edu/ency/article/000339.htm.

65. Hoyt, *Ghost of the Atlantic*, 109.

66. Ibid., 110.

67. Ibid., 114–15.

68. Ibid.

69. Ibid.

70. Hoyt, *Ghost of the Atlantic*, 112–13.

71. Niezychowski, *Cruise of the Kronprinz Wilhelm*, 300.

## *Chapter 2*

72. *New York Times*, March 10, 1915.

73. Ibid.

74. *Virginian-Pilot and the Norfolk Landmark*, March 11, 1915.

75. Ibid.

76. Ibid.

77. Ibid.

78. Ibid.

79. Edwin B. Parker, "Arthur Sewall and Company et al. (United States) v. Germany." Reports of International Arbitral Awards, Volume 7, April 21, 1926 (United Nations, 2006), 318.

80. Ibid., 318.

81. Ibid.

82. *Virginian-Pilot and the Norfolk Landmark*, March 18, 1915.

83. Ibid.

84. Ibid.

85. Ibid.

86. Ibid., March 15, 1915.

87. *Declaration Concerning the Laws of Naval War, 208 Consol. T.S.*, University of Minnesota, Human Rights Library, accessed June 26, 2017, http://hrlibrary.umn.edu/instree/1909b.htm.

88. Ibid., March 28, 1915.

89. Ibid.

90. Raphael Semmes, *My Adventures Afloat: A Personal Memoir of My Cruises and Services in 'The Sumter' and 'Alabama'* (London: Richard Bentley, 1869), 761–69.

91. *Virginian-Pilot and the Norfolk Landmark*, March 12, 1915.

92. Ibid.

93. Ibid.

94. Ibid.

95. Ibid., March 11, 1915.

96. Ibid., March 13, 1915.

97. Ibid.

98. Ibid.

99. Ibid.

100. Ibid., March 11, 1915

101. Ibid., March 29, 1915.

102. Ibid.

103. Ibid.
104. Ibid.
105. Ibid., March 18, 1915.
106. Ibid., March 13, 1915.
107. Ibid., March 11, 1915.
108. Ibid.
109. Ibid.
110. Ibid., March 12, 1915.
111. Ibid.
112. Ibid.
113. Ibid.
114. Ibid., May 10, 1915.

## *Chapter 3*

115. *Virginian-Pilot and the Norfolk Landmark*, April 4, 1915.
116. Ibid., April 15, 1915.
117. Ibid., April 23, 1915.
118. Thierichens to Sentries, December 5, 1915, NARA.
119. *Virginian-Pilot and the Norfolk Landmark*, March 14, 1915.
120. Ibid., March 15, 1915.
121. Ibid.
122. Ibid., March 21, 1915.
123. Ibid.
124. Ibid, March 28, 1915.
125. Ibid.
126. Ibid.
127. Ibid., April, 25, 1915.
128. Ibid., April 9, 1915.
129. Ibid.
130. Ibid., April 30, 1915.
131. Ibid.
132. Ibid., June 10, 1915.
133. Ibid.
134. Ibid., April 3, 1915.
135. Ibid.
136. Ibid., April 15, 1915.
137. Ibid.

138. Ibid.

139. Ibid., April 28, 1915.

140. Ibid.

141. Ibid., May 6, 1915.

142. Ibid., May 6, 1915.

143. Ibid., May 25, 1915.

144. Ibid.

145. Ibid., May 1, 1915.

146. Ibid., May 2, 1915.

147. U.S. Representative C.C. Holland to Rear Admiral Beatty, June 19, 1915, NARA.

148. Ibid.

149. *Virginian-Pilot and the Norfolk Landmark*, June 5, 1915.

150. Ibid.

151. Phyllis Ann Hall, "America's Great Little German Village at the Naval Shipyard in Portsmouth," in *Olde Times* (Portsmouth, VA: Olde Towne Ventures, Summer 1987), 1–9.

152. Ibid.

153. *Virginian-Pilot and the Norfolk Landmark*, August 27, 1916.

154. Hall, "America's Great Little German Village, 1–9.

155. Ibid., 2.

156. Ibid., 5.

157. Ibid.

## *Chapter 4*

158. Thierichens to Beatty, July 5, 1915, NARA.

159. *Virginian-Pilot and the Norfolk Landmark*, July 15, 1915.

160. Ibid.

161. Ibid., April 23, 1915.

162. Beatty to Thierichens, July 5, 1915, NARA.

163. McLean to Thierichens, May 9, 1916, NARA.

164. Ibid., May 10, 1916, NARA.

165. Ibid.

166. *Virginian-Pilot and the Norfolk Landmark*, May 3, 1915.

167. Thierichens to McLean, December 3, 1915, NARA.

168. *Virginian-Pilot and the Norfolk Landmark*, December 25, 1915.

169. Ibid.

170. Ibid.

171. Thierfelder to McLean, December 26, 1915, NARA.

172. H.L. Mencken, *Thirty-Five Years of Newspaper Work: A Memoir by H.L. Mencken* (Baltimore, MD: Johns Hopkins University Press, 1994), 57.

173. Ibid.

174. Ibid.

175. Thierfelder to McLean, December 20, 1916, NARA.

176. McLean to Thierichens, December 21, 1916, NARA.

177. Irwin M. Berent, *Norfolk Virginia: A Jewish History of the 20th Century* (Virginia Beach, VA: United Jewish Federation of Tidewater, 2001), 49.

178. Ibid., 50.

179. Ibid.

180. Ibid.

181. Ibid.

182. Ibid.

183. Beatty to Thierichens, November 5, 1915, NARA.

184. McLean to Thierichens, May 3, 1916, NARA.

185. Paul G. Halpern, *A Naval History of World War I* (Abingdon, UK: Routledge, 1994), 72.

186. Dan Van der Vat, *Gentleman of War: The Amazing Story of Captain Karl von Muller and the SMS Emden* (New York: William and Company, 1984), 48.

187. Thierichens to McLean, December 1915, NARA.

188. *New York Times*, February 3, 1916.

189. Thierichens to McLean, July 26, 1916, NARA.

190. Ibid.

191. Ibid.

192. Daniels to McLean, July 29, 1916, NARA.

193. Halpern, *Naval History of World War I*, 336.

194. Charles F. Horne, ed., "German Submarine Deutschland's Atlantic Crossing, 9 July 1916," in *Source Records of the Great War*, Volume 4 (New York: National Alumni, 1921).

195. *Virginian-Pilot and the Norfolk Landmark*, July 11, 1916.

196. Ibid., August 4, 1916.

197. Ibid., August 27, 1916.

198. Ibid.

199. *Kolonie-Anzeiger*, September 2, 1916.

200. Ibid.

## *Chapter 5*

201. *Virginian-Pilot and the Norfolk Landmark*, March 20, 1915.

202. Daniels to Beatty, June 10, 1915, NARA.

203. *Virginian-Pilot and the Norfolk Landmark*, March 20, 1915.

204. Ibid.

205. Ibid.

206. Cecil Spring-Rice to Daniels, October 15, 1915, NARA. Forward original letter from Frau Brauer to Curt Brauer, August 19, 1915.

207. Ibid.

208. Ibid.

209. Ibid.

210. Daniels to Beatty, November 5, 1915, NARA.

211. *Virginian-Pilot and the Norfolk Landmark*, June 12, 1915.

212. Beatty to Daniels, November 11, 1915, NARA.

213. *Virginian-Pilot and the Norfolk Landmark*, June 12, 1915.

214. Cecil Spring-Rice to Daniels, July 21, 1915, NARA.

215. W.P. Allen to Beatty, October 25, 1915, NARA.

216. Ibid.

217. Hamilton to McAdoo, September 29, 1915, NARA.

218. Beatty to Chief of Naval Operations Admiral William S. Benson, September 30, 1915, NARA.

219. Ibid.

220. *Virginian-Pilot and the Norfolk Landmark*, October 15, 1915.

221. Beatty to Daniels, October 13, 1915, NARA.

222. Thierfelder to Beatty, October 15, 1915, NARA.

223. Daniels to Beatty, November, 5, 1915, NARA.

224. Beatty to Daniels, interview with Thierfelder concerning *Eclipse* provisions, November, 5, 1915, NARA.

225. R.G. Thomas to Beatty, October 29, 1915, NARA.

226. Ibid.

227. *Virginian-Pilot and the Norfolk Advertiser*, October 23, 1915.

228. Clark Weaton to Beatty, October 27, 1915, NARA.

229. Chiswell to St. Helena Naval Training Station, October 20, 1915, NARA.

230. Daniels to Virginia Beach Naval Radio Compass Station, October 20, 1915, NARA.

231. W.P. Allen to Beatty, October 25, 1915, NARA.

232. Daniels to Virginia Beach Naval Radio Compass Station, October 20, 1915, NARA.

233. *New York Times*, October 19, 1915.
234. Beatty to Thierichens, October 15, 1915, NARA.
235. Roosevelt to Norfolk Navy Yard, October 15, 1915, NARA.
236. Beatty to Thierichens, October 30, 1915, NARA.
237. Ibid.
238. Beatty to Thierichens, October 30, 1915, NARA.
239. Red Cross Transport Commander to Beatty, October 27, 1915, NARA.
240. Beatty to Daniels, October 21, 1915, NARA.
241. Thierichens to Beatty, November 12, 1915, NARA.
242. Ibid., November 11, 1915.
243. Beatty to Detroit Chief of Police, November, 15, 1915, NARA (wireless radio communication).
244. Detroit Chief of Police to Beatty, November, 15, 1915, NARA (wireless radio communication).
245. Sheriff, Falls City, Nebraska, to Beatty, November 18, 1915, NARA.
246. Beatty to Sheriff, Falls City, Nebraska, November 22, 1915, NARA.
247. Daniels to McLean, December 2, 1915, NARA.
248. Otto Buelow to Daniels, December, 5, 1915, NARA.
249. Beatty to Thierichens, November 11, 1915, NARA.
250. Thierichens to Beatty, November 13, 1915, NARA.
251. Ibid., November 20, 1915, NARA.
252. Ibid.
253. Daniels to Beatty, November 22, 1915, NARA.

## *Chapter 6*

254. Ibid.
255. Ibid.
256. Ibid.
257. Ibid.
258. *Virginian-Pilot and the Norfolk Landmark*, November 26, 1915.
259. *New York Times*, March 21, 1930.
260. McLean to Daniels, December 1, 1915, NARA.
261. Ibid.
262. *Virginian-Pilot and the Norfolk Landmark*, November 29, 1915.
263. McLean to Daniels, November 29, 1915, NARA.
264. Senior Officer of Navy Afloat, E.A. Anderson to Commanding Officers of *Delaware* and *Vermont*, November 29, 1915, NARA.

265. Hoyt, *Ghost of the Atlantic*, 139.

266. Thierfelder to Beatty, May 27, 1915, NARA.

267. Ibid.

268. Senior Aid to Commandant C.J. Lacy to Thierfelder, May 28, 1915, NARA.

269. H.C. Snyder to Beatty and McLean, November 25, 1915, NARA.

270. Thierichens to McLean, December 8, 1915, NARA.

271. Ibid.

272. McLean to H.C. Snyder, December 9, 1915, NARA.

273. McLean to Thierfelder, July 24, 1916, NARA.

274. Lieutenant Mueller to McLean, November 1915, NARA.

275. Ibid.

276. Daniels to Beatty, November 13, 1915, NARA.

277. Thierichens to McLean, January 4, 1916, NARA.

278. Ibid., February 18, 1916, NARA.

279. McLean to Thierichens, November, 30, 1915, NARA.

280. Thierichens to Beatty, November 23, 1915, NARA.

281. McLean to Daniels, May 25, 1916, NARA.

282. Ibid.

283. McLean to Daniels, September, 9, 1916, NARA.

284. McLean to Daniels, August 7, 1916, NARA.

285. Ibid.

286. McLean to Thierichens, August, 9, 1916, NARA.

287. Ibid.

288. McLean to Daniels, September 2, 1916, NARA.

289. Hall, "America's Great Little German Village," 425.

## *Epilogue*

290. Hoyt, *Ghost of the Atlantic*, 139.

291. Ibid., 140.

292. Ibid., 141.

293. William B. Gidden, *Internment Camps in America, 1917–1920*, Volume 37, no. 4, December 1973 (Washington: D.C.: American Military Institute), 137–38.

294. Niezychowski, *The Cruise of the Kronprinz Wilhelm*, viii.

295. Woodrow Wilson: "Executive Order 2624—German Boats," May 22, 1917. Online by Gerhard Peters and John T. Woolley, *The American Presidency Project*, http://www.presidency.ucsb.edu/ws/?pid=75420.